What Health Care Professionals Say About *Babywise*

In the morass of recently published books on parenting, this exceedingly practical manual emerges as a beacon of guidance, wisdom, and common sense. Parents of all backgrounds will benefit from the time-tested methods presented. I have interacted with children raised in this method first-hand, and can attest to scores of well-adjusted children who are a joy to their parents. I wholeheartedly endorse this manual without reservation.

Jonathan L. Scott, M.D., Ph.D.
Los Angeles, California

Medical school in no way prepared me for one of the more demanding aspects of my practice: dealing with infant feeding. The theory of feeding a baby whenever it cries, which was standard teaching, was not only without justification—it simply did not meet the needs of my patients. Since being introduced to the principles of *Babywise*, I have been convinced of its effectiveness in establishing sleep patterns and in decreasing the frequency of problems associated with infant feeding. If thriving children and happy, rested parents were not enough, my greatest commendation of *Babywise* is that my own children are being raised by these precepts.

Craig Lloyd, M.D.
Brisbane, Australia

As a pediatrician, I cannot argue with the success of *Babywise*. It is such a practical approach to parenting. It provides infants with needed structure and stability and brings the joy and love so needed in our homes today. The effects of not using *Babywise* show up very quickly. That is why I have made these principles a priority of discussion in every well-child care visit. Parents constantly tell me, "It changed our lives."

Janet Dahmen, M.D.
Chatsworth, California

As an obstetrician and a mother, my concern for a healthy outcome continues beyond the moment of delivery. Because the principles of *Babywise* are so effective, I consider it part of my extended health care for the entire family. The principles are simple—yet amazing. They consistently produce babies who are healthy, content, and who sleep through

the night at an early age. Feeding a baby on demand simply cannot compare to the overall healthy benefits of *Babywise*. The concepts take the guesswork out of early parenting, and provide new moms the confidence of knowing what happens next. Not following the principles of *Babywise* is a potential health concern.

Sharon Nelson, M.D.
Glendale, California

As a clinical associate professor of obstetrics and gynecology, a certified nurse-midwife, childbirth educator, and a mom, I would be doing a disservice to my patients if I did not direct them to *Babywise*. The infant management theories of the last twenty-five years have been rendered useless in light of the tremendous success of this program. Why would any parent not want a happy, healthy, and content baby who sleeps through the night in the first two months? Why would any parent not desire the confidence *Babywise* offers? *Babywise* provides wisdom, common sense, confidence—all refreshing and hopeful words for expectant parents to feast upon.

Diane Dirks, C.N.M.
Pasadena, California

I am a practicing pediatrician and assistant professor of pediatrics. Residents and new mothers I work with have found *Babywise* overwhelmingly successful. My residents report a positive difference in the confidence of new mothers who work with this plan compared to those who do not. The freedom *Babywise* provides a new mother is so refreshing. Life is predictable, allowing her to be proactive in parenting, not reactive, which usually produces less than desirable results. My parents become baby wise with *Babywise*.

Linda Meloy, M.D.
Richmond, Virginia

As a mother, I have parented both ways. As a certified lactation educator, I only recommend *Babywise*. I know how discouraging it is to feed a baby around the clock with no apparent advantage. I know how tired a young mom can get and how that affects her milk supply. I also know how discouraging the first eighteen months of parenting can be without a plan. I know because with my first child I did everything the opposite of *Babywise*. Before my second baby was born, I was introduced to the concepts presented in this book. Applying the principles revolutionized my thinking. Instead of being in baby bondage, I was liberated to be the mother God wanted me to be. I have consistently used *Babywise* with the women I counsel. These mothers have met with tremendous success, whether bottle or breast-feeding. *Babywise* is proactive, preventative parenting, minimizing the common problems often associated with breast-feeding.

Barbara Phillips, R.N., C.L.E.
Los Angeles, California

As a practicing pediatrician, husband, and father, I enthusiastically recommend *Babywise.* I found the principles contained within to be a sigh of welcome relief to sleepless, weary parents, and more than an ounce of prevention for those who adopt these concepts from the start. I am convinced that the well-tested principles of *Babywise* produce confident parents, secure and content infants, and peaceful and orderly homes.

David Blank, M.D.
Longmont, Colorado

As family physicians and a husband-wife team, we are often asked questions related to parenting and the general care of children. Most of our basic responses are found in *Babywise.* For answering parenting questions, it has become a practical guide giving us a sense of competence and confidence as physicians and as parents. When the principles are put into practice, parents reap abundant rewards.

Tony Burden, M.D., and Margaret Burden, M.D.
Bellingham, Washington

What Moms and Dads Are Saying About *Babywise*

My sister-in-law gave me *Babywise* when my baby was three months old. I had read lots and lots of books and magazines, talked to many experienced mothers, and asked the help of my pediatrician, but nothing had answered all of my questions—until I read your book. I highly recommend this book to all mothers and mothers-to-be.

A mother from West Covina, California

My husband and I had heard all sorts of horror stories and felt so discouraged and defeated before our baby came. Feeding around the clock, unexplained fussiness, and bondage (to our baby) was not what we wanted. We were sure there had to be a more sane way to parent than that. We were introduced to your concepts a week after our son was born. How timely! As predicted, our baby was sleeping through the night at five weeks. We have order in our family and are not ashamed of it. Thank you for giving us the confidence to do what is best for our son.

A mother from Denver, Colorado

Without reservation I would recommend this program to anyone—because it works. I demand-fed my first three children, not knowing there was another way. I didn't get a complete night's sleep in five years. When friends began to share your principles, I refused to listen to what I thought was simplistic nonsense. I hold a master's degree in Early Childhood Education and your concepts challenged everything I was taught.

When our friends' first child slept through the night at six weeks, I was enraged. My husband and I watched as their second and third followed the same pattern. They had everything under control, and so few of the problems that we experienced. When I discovered that I was expecting baby number four, I was depressed for months. The only thing I could focus on was the misery of more sleepless nights and demanding children.

I am ashamed to say that it was out of desperation that we applied your Parent-Directed Feeding. I was humbled. Our baby slept through the night at four weeks. We couldn't believe it was that easy. He was a delight, happy and content, something never experienced with the first three. Since then, a fifth child has arrived and, again, success. *Babywise* has saved our marriage and family. Thank you.

A mother from Philadelphia, Pennsylvania

My husband and I want to thank you for getting us on the right track from the beginning. It wasn't easy, because all our friends followed the demand-feeding philosophy and said a schedule was bad for the baby. For these families, children were a major interruption. That didn't make sense to us. We stayed with your program and our baby slept eight hours through the night at six weeks, and eleven hours at twelve weeks—just like your book says. My friends said exactly what you predicted: that we were lucky and had an easy baby. But we know otherwise. Thank you for being a source of encouragement.

A mother from Fort Worth, Texas

I was at church holding a crying baby and everyone asked what was wrong with my son. They said they had never before heard him cry. Then they realized it wasn't my son I was holding. Thank you for *Babywise*. My wife and I have a happy, contented baby.

Before our son was born we'd heard so many sad stories. My sister had not gone out with her husband alone for three years after the birth of their first son. She went to a mothers' support group but only found other mothers to cry with. No thank you. Not for my wife. We follow the principles of PDF. Because our lives are so predictable and our son responds so well to routine, we had our first date-night after three weeks and once a week ever since. Thank you for helping to keep our family a family.

A father from Tacoma, Washington

Our daughter will be one year old at the end of this month and I must tell you that I truly and profoundly enjoyed this year of her life. A big part of the reason is because we followed the principles of *Babywise*. It was not only helpful with my daughter, but also helped me understand my frustrations with my first born! I kept wondering why he was so demanding. Why would he never sleep at night or take decent naps?

I had nursed my son as often as he needed (so I thought)—anytime and anywhere, day and night—until he was twenty-two months old.

And I gave him attention, both quality and quantity. He slept with us at night but after a few weeks the baby slept with only me at night; my husband was on the couch. I stayed home, gave him a good learning environment, and cooked all natural foods. I did everything the "experts" said to do. But they were so wrong. In the end, it was all for nothing. The only thing I succeeded in doing was to raise a demanding, out-of-control toddler who is not pleasant to be with.

I don't share this to burden you, but to encourage you. Please get the *Babywise* principles out to young families of our nation (Canada) and yours, so they will not have to suffer what we did. Thank you for your sensible teaching.

A mother from Vancouver, British Columbia

My husband and I want to thank you for helping us gain the confidence to parent. Your book has been around to all the expectant moms at our preschool. Everyone wants to know why our son, Jonathan, is such a good baby. My husband and I have found parenting to be a joyful experience. It makes so much sense to work from a plan and provide order for our child. Because of that, I have more energy for my husband, my friends, and to do the extra things with my son. Thank you.

A mother from Los Angeles, California

My wife and I were introduced to your program while in marriage counseling. It was then that we discovered the trap of child-centered parenting. In the name of "good parenthood," we gave up our marriage—figuratively and nearly literally. We did this for the "baby's good." That sounded sacrificial and was something I wanted to do as a father. But I never realized how faulty that thinking was until I read your first two chapters. Your book makes sense out of nonsense.

After eighteen months of misery, we started our son on a routine. After three nights he began sleeping through the night and my wife began to sleep with me—but this time alone. What a difference a good night's sleep makes to a toddler's disposition! We had a new son. Get these vital principles out to every family of childbearing age.

A father from Atlanta, Georgia

I am a grandmother with fourteen grandchildren. I must admit, the evidence of your principles is apparent in our family. My second daughter was introduced to your material in Florida and brought it back to the rest of the family. I was surprised that your teaching is needed. You tell parents to do what we did years ago when there were no books or tapes, just practical wisdom. Thank you for your practical advice. You have helped make grandparenting a joy.

A grandmother from Raleigh, North Carolina

Thank you so much for your book. What an eye opener! With the utmost love and the best intentions, I had gone wrong in most ways with regard to feeding/sleeping patterns and breast feeding. I followed the demand-feeding methodology. How deceived I was. Your book arrived at a point of desperation, with our baby waking eight to twelve times nightly and a four-year-old coming into our bed each night. Existing on almost no sleep, our marriage was suffering and we both decided we couldn't live this way anymore. A counselor pointed us to *Babywise*. It turned our lives around. Please use this letter to encourage young couples to grasp and hold on to the principles of *Babywise*.

A mother from Christ Church, New Zealand

ON BECOMING

BABY WISE

BOOK ONE

*How 100,000 new parents trained
their babies to sleep through
the night the natural way*

■

GARY EZZO AND
ROBERT BUCKNAM, M. D.

MULTNOMAH BOOKS

ON BECOMING BABYWISE

published by Multnomah Books
a part of the Questar publishing family

© 1995 by Gary Ezzo and Robert Bucknam, M.D.

International Standard Book Number: 0-88070-909-X

Edited by Stephen T. Barclift

Designed by David Carlson

Cover photo by David Hanover, Tony Stone Images

Printed in the United States of America

For information:
QUESTAR PUBLISHERS, INC.
POST OFFICE BOX 1720
SISTERS, OREGON 97759

97 98 99 00 01 02 — 10 9

To:
Dr. Fred and Mary Barshaw—
for their many years
of lighting the way.

ACKNOWLEDGMENTS

We owe a special debt of gratitude to Dr. Eleanor Womack, a Harvard-trained physician who is now mother of triplets. Due to her first-hand experience and expertise, we asked Dr. Womack if she would write for us a chapter dealing with multiple births. She consented, and we are very grateful for her help. (See Chapter 10, "Multiple Birth: The Endless Party.") We also wish to thank author Gary Ezzo's wife, Anne Marie, for her contribution to this book. Her background in pediatric nursing and childbirth education, and her partnership with Gary in Growing Families International, have made her an invaluable asset to this project.

CONTENTS

FOREWORD

After completing medical school and serving my residency in obstetrics and gynecology, I felt knowledgeable enough to be a parent. Between my wife's degree in child development and my medical training, how hard could this parenting thing be? We would just do what comes naturally and follow our instincts. Right? Wrong!

Soon after the birth of our first son, we quickly found that our enthusiasm and confidence had turned into exhaustion and frustration. Mom was up three times at night and the baby was cranky during the day. The unsolicited advice typically offered was to feed the baby more often since he obviously was hungry. We did feed him, around the clock, every two hours. So much for instincts!

Scientists can put a man on the moon, but they have not been able to answer this basic question of early parenting: How can I have a happy and contented baby, who sleeps continually through the night like the rest of the family, and be a mother (or father) who is not in a perpetual state of exhaustion?

Through our common interest in children and parenting, my wife and I became acquainted with the work and accomplishments of Gary and Anne Marie Ezzo of *Growing Families International*. The Ezzo's basic and loving concepts for nurturing newborns virtually eliminated the problems mentioned above, and many more. I have personally observed both infants who were guided by the Ezzo's principles and those who were not. It became obvious that parents equipped with the right information do make a difference.

I have since made the transition from obstetrics to pediatrics, and with the switch came the medically sound principles of *Babywise*.

They work consistently, not only for the thousands of children already touched by *Growing Families International*, but also for my three children, my colleagues' children, my friends' children, and now, for all my patients.

To say the least, *Babywise* has brought a needed reformation to pediatric counsel given to new parents. When parents come in looking exhausted and discouraged and tell me their woeful stories of sleepless nights and fussy babies, I can give them a positive prescription that cures the problem—I hand them a copy of *Babywise*.

Robert Bucknam, M.D.

INTRODUCTION

Yes, one day people will stop you on the street or at the grocery store and comment, "Your baby is so content." Then they will insult you with the following commentary: "You're so lucky to have such an easy baby. What? Sleeping through the night already? How old is she? You're *very* fortunate!"

As philosopher Immanuel Kant pointed out, the actual proves the possible. With *Babywise*, we no longer count the success stories in thousands, but in tens of thousands. *Babywise* isn't a book of luck but of principles. Chance has nothing to do with the benefits described above—right parenting does. What you do in the first days, weeks, and months of your baby's life will impact all the rest of your parenting years.

This is more than a sleep-training book. Getting your baby to sleep through the night within six to eight weeks is the easiest part of parenting. Realizing the awesome duty of raising a responsible human being is more difficult.

This book will not provide you with a list of rules. We wish parenting were that easy. Our purpose is to get you started on the right track, beginning with the preparation of your mind, which is far more important than preparation of the nursery. Your baby will not care if his head rests on designer sheets or on Disney characters. His behavior will not be ordered by his wardrobe or by his bedroom accessories, but by the mind-set that dictates how you live your life.

Our personal perspective of life in general governs how we relate to our children, to our spouse, and to others. This book assumes that the reader is family-centered and is not child-centered. That means you regard your baby as a welcome member of the family and not the center of the family universe. That perspective is foundational to the concepts presented in this book.

In discussing infant and maternal physiology, we will demonstrate how order and stability are mutual allies of every newborn's metabolism. In particular, we will discuss how an infant's body responds to the influences of parental routine, or the lack thereof.

In the final chapters, we will examine day-to-day aspects of infant management. Included is a description of the three basic elements of daytime activities for newborns: feeding time, waketime, and naptime.

The questions at the end of most chapters will explore the key themes found in your reading. We encourage you to take the time to read the questions and write out the answers. You will feel more confident as a parent when you know *what* to do and *why* you should do it. We designed the study questions to serve as an aid in gaining that confidence.

Babywise is more than an infant-management concept; it is a strategy for responsible parenthood. The principles presented will help any parent develop a plan that meets both the needs of a new baby and of the entire family. This plan will not leave mom ragged at the end of the day, nor in bondage to her child. And dad won't be excluded from his duties, either. These principles have worked for thousands of parents and, when faithfully applied, will also work wonderfully for you!

Gary Ezzo

....

Chapter One

Your Baby
Needs a Family

*B*ecause the family is the primary social unit of every society, it is also the most important—one worth protecting and keeping. As professionals providing health and educational services to children and parents, we know the tragedy that can befall a family when basic principles of parenting are violated. We have counseled parents who started with the best intentions to love and nurture their children, only to see their dreams of a beautiful family reduced to a nightmare of survival. The problem is not one of wrong motives, but wrong methods.

There are two related dangers that threaten successful parenting. The first is not rightly understanding the significance of the husband-wife relationship in the parenting process, and the second is the danger of child-centered parenting.

We believe that the best possible set of parenting circumstances includes a husband and wife who are committed to each other, and the husband-wife team is the model upon which much of the book's material is based. However, if you are a single parent, or your spouse is absent from the home, don't assume this book isn't for you. Your job as parent may be more difficult, but the principles presented in this and subsequent chapters are universally true, and can be applied in all families.

The Greatest Influence: The Husband-Wife Relationship

The greatest overall influence you will have on your children will not come in your role as an individual, but in your joint role as husband and wife. This basic truth is often forgotten, resulting in a society consumed with child-centeredness, self-centeredness, and quests for self-fulfillment. Emotional and physical harm to children is the ultimate consequence of our neglect.

As professionals, we cannot overstate how necessary a healthy husband-wife relationship is to the emotional well-being of children. Frequently, parents lose sight of the fact that when their children enter the family, they enter an established social structure. Parents often act as if the marriage union were only a preliminary relationship to child rearing, rather than perceiving it as an ongoing priority relationship.

Maintaining the marriage relationship as a priority is necessary for successful parenting. The quality of the parent-child relationship depends upon the quality of the husband-wife relationship.

At this time we would like to introduce two fictional characters who will appear at various times throughout this book. Their names are Chelsea and Marisa—cousins born within a week of each other. Chelsea's parents followed the principles presented in this book; Marisa's parents did not. Although these are fictional characters, the differences stated in their development are factual.

Of all Chelsea's emotional needs, her most basic one is knowing her world is secure. What she observes between her mom and dad establishes that sense of security. As she observes their emotional togetherness in the normal course of a day, she is more secure simply because she does not have to question the legitimacy of their commitment to one another.

All children are born with a radar device that hones in on parental conflict. If a child perceives more weakness than strength, it produces a low-level anxiety that ultimately affects his or her ability to learn. A child knows intuitively, just as the child's parents knew when they were growing up, that if something happens to mom and dad, his or her whole world will collapse. If the parents' relationship is always in question in the mind of a child, then the child will live his or her life on the brink of disaster.

Chelsea's mom can spend twenty-four hours a day loving and nurturing her, but all that sacrificial time and attention can never meet Chelsea's need to know that her mom loves her dad. Her dad can buy all sorts of toys and play with her for hours, but that will not satisfy the greatest desire of Chelsea's heart: to know that her dad and mom love each other.

When a child has confidence in his or her parents' relationship, that child is emotionally free to get on with life. When there is harmony in the husband-wife relationship, there is stability within the family. Strong marriages provide a haven of security for children as they grow.

Child-Centered Parenting

Often, in the name of good parenting, moms and dads leave their first love—each other—and focus totally, or nearly so, on their children. That refocusing is the first step to the breakup of the family,

21

leading to the second threat to successful parenting: the belief that children are to be the center of the family universe.

Marisa's parents believe that way. As a result, they are willing to gamble the future of the whole family. They base their practice on the belief that good parenting is determined solely by the amount of attention and sacrifice given to children. Marisa will never have to wait for anything. If she cries, her parents will pick her up immediately. If she wants something, she will get it. There will be no baby-sitters for Marisa. If she can't go with her parents, they don't go. If she doesn't like her baby food, no problem; her mom will offer a variety of choices until she finds something Marisa likes.

Marisa's parents don't realize that all their good intentions are fostering an emotional disability we call *me-ism*. Marisa's perception of her place in life depends significantly on the feedback and stimulation she receives from the people around her. If that stimulation is such that it leads her to perceive herself to be the center of the family, she will develop a self-centered perception that will carry into every relationship she forms as her world expands.

We have seen the devastating results of that style of parenting. Marisa's potential for failure in basic relationships will increase because other people simply will not matter to her. She will have difficulty getting along with siblings and peers. She will grow up ill-prepared for real life, where the ability to give and take is a prerequisite for healthy and enduring relationships. Because other significant people in her life will not cater to her as quickly as her mom and dad do, life for Marisa will become terribly frustrating.

By contrast, Chelsea's mom and dad are raising her with an eye toward integrating her life into the already existing family structure.

They are creating within their daughter an inclination to develop close and loving relationships. When a child perceives herself as a welcome member of the family, she gradually learns to integrate into other social relationships with flexibility and confidence. For any child, being a welcome member of the family produces a *we-ism* attitude. That attitude accepts one's role in the family as a team member—where giving is as important as receiving.

Friendship and Conformity

Chelsea's parents believe they are obligated to produce a responsible human being, and they are not willing to leave that goal to chance. They accept the challenge of parenting, realizing the process of training begins with *them*. For Chelsea, belonging to her family is not an option, but a mandate. Her parents expect certain behaviors of her and are willing to force conformity when required. They believe there are certain virtues worth acquiring—such as kindness, goodness, gentleness, charity, honesty, honor, and respect for others.

Since these qualities are not naturally found in Chelsea's tiny little life, they must be nurtured into her heart. Chelsea's parents accept their role as loving governors. That is, they will govern her life until they have developed within her heart the self-control and moral awareness that will allow her to govern herself. That freedom comes gradually—from the playpen to the back yard, and then to the neighborhood. As Chelsea demonstrates responsible behavior and sound judgment, she earns another level of freedom. That type of training results in a child who is a joy to everyone, and one who achieves a sense of affirmation within herself.

In contrast, Marisa's mom and dad are following a different philosophy of parenting. They believe good parenting only requires them to be friends with their child, so they treat her as a peer. Unfortunately, no one informed them of the consequences of such thinking. With that style of parenting, family relationships for Marisa will always be optional.

This theory of child-rearing, called *democratic parenting*[1] is based on making everyone equal in the family, in the hope that doing so will somehow eliminate all naughty behavior from the life of the child.[2] Marisa's mom and dad act more like her buddies than her parents, even banishing from their family the two terms of endearment that are so special in the life of every little boy and girl, *"Daddy"* and *"Mommy."* Instead, using their first names is acceptable: Marisa will simply call them Bob and Sue.

Who would not want to be friends with their children? From a parenting perspective, what can sound more noble or captivating than a family made up of friends? Certainly that is an admirable idea, especially appealing to a generation who may have wondered about the lack of friendship with their own parents. But is it right?

When parents remove terms of endearment (and the relationships they represent) from a child's life, they sever a major strand that ties together close relationships. Maybe this separation is one reason democratic parenting has failed over the past twenty years. That fact may also explain why our society saw a proliferation of teenage rebellion and broken families in the 1970s and 1980s.

Being your child's friend is not the starting point of your parenting, but the relational goal. Friendship is what you are attempting to achieve by the end of the teen years. Of course you will still have fun with your children. You *can* be buddies during the training process. But successful parenting requires that a parent not devalue his or her role, reducing it to the level of the child. Neither should a parent elevate the child to the level of a peer.

Time and experience are prerequisites for building any friendship. Children are not born with the benefit of having wisdom, experience, or self-control. Once you became a parent, you became responsible for training your child. Nature automatically grants you the right to make decisions in your child's best interest.

Responsible parenthood means you are the teacher and your children are the students. You lead, they follow. There will be plenty of time for friendship later, and with responsible parenting, plenty of reason for it.

By proxy, Chelsea's parents represent her best interests. As her mother and father, they know what is best for her and will insist on compliance. For Chelsea, family relationships have meaning and purpose. She belongs to something bigger than herself—she belongs to her family.

Achieving a Balance

Becoming child-centered is easy when you have a baby. Infants are totally dependent on parental care, and that heightens the gratification of the parenting experience. However, there are ways that you can meet all your baby's needs and not be child-centered. Here are a few ideas that can help you achieve that balance:

1. *Remind yourself that life doesn't stop once you have a baby.* It may slow down for a few weeks, but it does not stop completely. When

you become a mother, you do not stop being a daughter, a sister, a friend, or a wife. Those relationships were important to you before the baby was born. Be sure to maintain them afterward.

2. *Date your spouse.* If you had a weekly date night with your spouse before the baby was born, continue that practice as soon as you can, letting friends or relatives watch the baby. A child does not go through separation anxiety when mom is out with dad. If you didn't have a weekly date night before baby's arrival, start now. Your date doesn't have to be expensive, or require a late evening.

3. *Continue doing those special things for each other that you did before children came into your lives.* If there was a favorite activity you both enjoyed previously, work it into your schedule. If a husband brings home a gift for the baby, he should also bring flowers for his wife. The idea here is basic: Continue making those loving gestures that have characterized your relationship up to now; keep it special.

4. *Invite friends over for a meal or for an evening of fellowship.* By focusing on these times of hospitality, you are forced to focus on your home. That distraction is healthy because it obligates you to plan your child's day around serving other people.

5. *Practice "couch time."* When the workday is over, take fifteen minutes and sit on the couch together as a couple. This should take place when the children are still up, not after they are in bed. Explain to them, "No unnecessary interruptions are allowed because this is Mommy and Daddy's special time together. Daddy will play with Chelsea afterward, but Mommy comes first." Couch time provides a visual expression of your togetherness. In this tangible way, a child can measure his or her mommy and daddy's love relationship and have that inner need satisfied. In addition, couch time provides a

consistent opportunity for a couple to share their relational needs with each other.

Summary

We desire that your family life be filled with joy, that it abound in sweet memories, and be untainted by regret. That's not a statement of idealism, but one of direction and encouragement. Priority relationships are not arbitrary. They are not dictated by circumstances or by social fads. Relationships within the family function best when parents orchestrate them to the common goal of love and family unity.

If you desire to achieve excellence in parenting, you must protect your marriage. A strong marriage acts as the stabilizing factor against the shocks of life. As you maintain that priority relationship, you are simultaneously hedging against child-centered parenting. The relationship you have with your child should be that of parent, teacher, and governor. He or she is not your peer, but someone who needs your guiding hand. From the beginning, your child is a welcome member of the family but never the center of it.

Finally, work toward the goal of your child's friendship, remembering this isn't the starting point of your relationship, but the objective.

Questions for Review

1. Of all Chelsea's primary emotional needs, which is the most basic?

2. What happens when a child perceives weakness in his or her parents' relationship?

3. What is the first step to breaking up a family?

4. What emotional disability does child-centered parenting produce?

5. How long should parents act as governors in the lives of their children?

6. The theory of democratic parenting is based on what two assumptions?

7. What is the role of friendship in the parenting process?

Chapter Two

Feeding Philosophies

a person might suppose that establishing good feeding habits would be the easiest feature of child training, since the drive to obtain nourishment is one of the strongest in all living creatures. But much more occurs during your baby's feeding time than just filling up a little tummy. Your choice in parenting philosophy will actually determine your child's hunger patterns, sleep patterns, and even his or her basic disposition.

Defining the Terms

New and expectant parents can easily become confused over the terminology associated with today's ever-expanding feeding philosophies. During your pregnancy, you may have been encouraged to *demand-feed* your new arrival, while at the same time warned not to follow a schedule, especially if you intend to breast-feed. Maybe you heard about a *demand schedule* or a *self-demand schedule*. Perhaps you were told to consider *natural feeding* for your baby, or to avoid *hyper-scheduling* because that is *rigid feeding*, and rigid feeding is not as good as *cry feeding*. Yet, cry feeding is supposedly less desirable than *cue feeding*, which is similar to *responsive feeding*. And what about bottle feeding? Is this a new twentieth-century concept practiced only by the modern mother?

Where did all those terms come from, and what do they mean? By reviewing social and historical feeding practices, we can gain insight into the philosophy, methodology, and even the mythology associated with infant feeding.

Prior to this century, common sense was the rule for raising children, not theoretical concepts. Mothers nursed their babies when they were hungry, but with guidance. The mother guided the hunger cycles of the baby to match her routine for care of the entire family. Mothers of the past were not clock watchers; they didn't have to be. They had a natural schedule set by their domestic duties. Routine and predictable feeding periods fit into a schedule that met the needs of their baby and those of the entire family. It was that simple.

As the industrial revolution progressed, new infant-management theories evolved. During this century, two theories have dominated American parenting. The first was introduced in the early years by a group of scientists called *behaviorists*, who acted on the assumption that a child would become what his or her environment dictated. They placed a greater emphasis on outward structure than on developing emotions and feelings. The belief among behaviorists was that controlled environments produced controlled emotions.

In the early 1920s, the American mother was introduced to a form of infant feeding called hyperscheduling or *clock feeding*. It established a strict four-hour feeding schedule, and mothers followed it to the minute. If a baby appeared hungry after three hours, too bad—he would just have to wait until the fourth hour. The clock was the final authority on feeding times, regardless of the needs of the baby or the mother.[1]

By the mid-1940s, a second theory, an adaptation of Sigmund Freud's child-rearing theories, started to nudge out the rigidity of behaviorism. Freud's twentieth-century followers stressed the instinctive, animal-like qualities of infancy as the starting point for child management.

Structure was not as important to those theorists as were the child's developing emotions. With revisions made to Freud's theories, the American parent was pulled to the other extreme. Now when the baby cried, he or she was to be fed immediately, whether hungry or not. It was postulated that nursing would satisfy both nutritional and presumed psychological needs.

To what type of psychological need were these theorists referring? Psychoanalysts attempted to locate the origin and nature of adult neuroses by discovering, through psychoanalysis, significant traumatic experiences in early childhood. Originally, the quest into the past ended in the preschool years (two or three years of age). When no traumatic experiences were found in the average patient, analysts were forced to either abandon their theory or, by faith, move to the conclusion that the original source of traumatic experience was the birthing process itself, as postulated by Austrian psychoanalyst Otto Rank in 1929. Even Freud greeted such a notion with skepticism.

It was hypothesized that lodged in a child's subconscious memory is the trauma of birth, which separated the infant from pleasurable union with his or her mother. As a result of the birth shock, the child has an unconscious yearning to return to the safety and security of the womb. Since it is presumed that the child remains psychologically fragile for the first two or three years of life, the mother's job is to create a constant womb-like environment that will protect the child.

That belief inspired the *neoprimitivistic* school of child care in the 1940s. This theory postulates that the separation at birth momentarily interrupts the mother-child *in utero* harmony. Therefore, the goal of early parenting is to reestablish that harmony. How is this supposed to be achieved? Only by the constant, day-and-night presence and availability of the mother to the child. New mothers are instructed to do whatever it takes to neutralize the supposed trauma of birth in order to offset its effects. The birth-trauma theory suffered from lack of objective verifiable data and was dismissed by 1949, only to resurface twenty-five years later repackaged, with some slight modifications, under the title *attachment parenting*.

As a result of that speculation, the American mother in the early 1950s was nudged to a nonstructured approach to parenting. First, Dr. Benjamin Spock rightly rejected behaviorists' assumptions of absolute structure and moved his patients toward structure mixed with flexibility. Authorizing mothers to use flexibility in their schedule was a radical concept in the 1950s—and a needed course correction. By 1970, Spock's views were pushed out by the practice of *feeding on demand*. The baby's cry replaced the clock and a parent-guided, flexible routine.

There are two basic requirements of the theory of feeding on demand. First, parents must assume that baby knows best, and reject any type of parent-guided routine. Second, they must accept the belief that the signal for food is the baby's cry, and that *every* cry is a request for food (or, as borrowed from the birth-trauma theory, a request for psychological comfort).

We would add a strong caution to those tempted to embrace the beliefs of the demand-feeding theory just described. Some newborns may not cry to signal hunger readiness for five to six hours, and crying is not always a signal of hunger. Weak and sickly babies may not have the energy to cry, so a demand-feeding approach could allow serious medical problems to go unnoticed that would otherwise be picked up with routine feedings.

> NOTE: From this point forward, when we refer to the practice of demand-feeding, we are referring to the following belief of those who hold to this theory: The cry of a baby is the primary signal for nursing, whether it be for food or a presumed psychological need, regardless of how much time has elapsed since the last nursing period.

By the early 1980s, the neoprimitivistic school of infant care and its attachment theories gained more ground. What the modern version proposes is remarkably similar to the 1940s version, when theorists told mothers to carry their babies endlessly, sleep with them, breast-feed them day and night without regard to any routine, and breast-feed them well into their second, third, or fourth year of life. The child, not the mother, was to initiate weaning, which means the child could be as old as four or even five before giving up nursing. Toilet training was to take place very late, perhaps not until the child decided voluntarily to become potty trained. Parents exalted the child as the center of the family universe and fashioned their parenting practices in such a way that they would avoid conflict, anxiety, and discomfort—to prevent the child from growing up with a debilitating psychosis. (Actually, if you parent this way, you *yourself* may end up with some form of psychosis.)

Attachment theorists subscribe to the doctrine of *felt needs* as the cue for care and training. Demand-feeding and immediate gratification are primary parts of the attachment process. These theories suggest that the sensitivity that helps a mother do the right thing at the right time develops more quickly (and to a greater degree) through nursing. They claim that this is why you supposedly can never nurse too long or too often. All wants are to be interpreted as needs. That explains why the devout attachment mother will respond to her baby's cry even if it is the third time in twenty minutes; she is acting on the conviction that her child is signaling her with an unpleasant emotion, one that must be dealt with, and one only she can satisfy. The possibility that her baby is just settling down and doesn't need another interruption from mom is out of the question. Justified in her thinking by the statement, "Every cry is to be interpreted as a need for breast food or breast comfort," she moves dutifully toward her child, *never realizing that her child's lack of contentment is the result of her parenting style.*

That strategy is carried into the toddler and post-toddler years. When a three-year-old boy signals for a snack by pulling on his mother's blouse, and his mother offers him the breast, even if only for a minute, the mother is acting on the belief that he still has an attachment need. According to the theory, to say no is to deny him love when he needs it.[2]

Possibly the child does have a need. But is it the result of birth trauma or a philosophy of parenting? Might the methods used to manufacture a secure attachment child be an essential part of the problem? Could the results be so obvious that we fail to see the forest for the trees? The kind of close interaction and involvement associated with demand-style parenting works against a child's good development. These theorists give no thought to the possibility that they are actually training mothers to misinterpret their baby's cues. As a result, the parenting style and not the throw of the genetic dice is responsible for producing the symptoms of the emotionally stressed *high-need* baby. Those symptoms include: a combination of excessive fussiness and colic-like symptoms; instability in feeding and sleep cycles; waking throughout the night for up to two years; perpetual need for comfort nursing; fear of mother separation; fear of sleeping by himself; desire for immediate gratification; lack of self-comforting coping skills; limited self-play adeptness; a demanding pretoddler and toddler; and one tired mom. How tragic. With all sincerity and unmatched sacrifice, these mothers, in hopes of meeting every need of their psychologically fragile child, too often create such a child.

The weakness of the birth-trauma theory, from birth to weaning, is found in its premise. Does the birthing process create psychologically fragile children? It's doubtful that newborns experience anxiety as a result of birth or have any memory of it at all. Neither conscious nor unconscious memory function can take place in the low-oxygen environment of the uterus. Memory function and synapse development depend on the brain receiving highly oxygenated blood, which comes from breathing. Breathing cannot begin until the lungs inflate, and that occurs after birth. In addition, higher brain centers are still developing at the time of birth.

For the sake of argument, let's assume there is the possibility of a functioning memory in the prebirth state. If we were to attribute wishes, hopes, and fears to the unborn, we would have to assume that toward the end of the pregnancy the child longs to be born, since his or her environment is no longer a paradise. The squirming, turning, wrenching, jerking, and kicking in the last month forces the assumption that the child is more eager to be freed from this environment than longing to stay in it. The womb restrains and holds the baby back from liberation.

What about the memories of restraint created in the last month? Do they produce a reservoir of anxiety? Could womb confinement be the original source of trauma? Is any of the above possible? Once you open the door of speculation regarding memory function in a prebirth state, all sorts of logical (yet bizarre) theories are possible.

Neoprimitivistic and attachment parenting theories are not well-grounded on an impeccable body of evidence. Hopeful speculation abounds, based upon a very small amount of objective and verifiable information. To date, no one has demonstrated a relationship between the birthing experience and subsequent neurosis.

While behaviorists emphasize outward structure and not the inner person, the neoprimitivistic school emphasizes the inner person at the expense of outward structure. As professionals, we believe both approaches are extreme, wrong, and detrimental to the healthy development of a baby and soon-to-be toddler.

We offer an alternative parenting philosophy that enables parents to provide structure while meeting all the developing needs of their baby. *Parent-directed feeding* (PDF) is an infant-management strategy designed to meet the nutritional, physical, and emotional needs of the baby, as well as the needs of the entire family.

Our premises are basic. First, we believe that when a woman becomes a mother, she doesn't stop being a wife, daughter, sister, friend, or neighbor. Second, our conviction is that a baby should be fed when he or she signals readiness. With PDF, a mother feeds her baby when the baby is hungry, but she takes advantage of the first few weeks of life to guide the baby's hunger patterns by a basic routine. This is *cooperative* parenting. Because routine feedings wonderfully influence the hunger metabolism of an infant, the mother guides feeding times for her baby to meet the baby's needs, as well as those of the entire family. Both parent and child cooperate in this effort. Because the child is a welcome member and not the center of the family, and because he or she is not as emotionally fragile as attachment theorists believe, everyone wins—baby, mother, father, and the sometimes forgotten siblings.

Unlike the variations of the neoprimitivistic theories discussed in this chapter, PDF assumes that parents already have the wisdom they need to direct their babies' feeding. You will learn more about this in the chapters which follow.

Questions for Review

1. During this century, what were the two predominant views of infant management? What did they emphasize?

2. What is the birth-trauma theory? What does it require from a mother?

3. What are two basic assumptions inherent in the title *feeding on demand?*

    a.

    b.

4. List some symptoms of the emotionally-stressed *high-need* baby.

5. List the two basic premises of *parent-directed feeding.*

    a.

    b.

Chapter Three

The Benefits of Order

*a*nyone seeking to understand the value of an infant routine must first free his or her mind from two popular misconceptions. One is the assumption that an infant routine detracts from meeting a baby's physical and emotional needs, and that somehow the word *schedule* is not compatible with the words *love, caring,* and *concern.* The second misconception is that an infant fed on demand will be happier, healthier, and generally more secure than the one fed by routine, because his parents continuously and immediately respond to his cries without question. In both cases, nothing could be further from the truth.

Parent-Directed Feeding (PDF)

As a parent, you will want to pursue a course that is best for your baby. That course includes paying attention to your baby's need for outward structure and attention to his developing emotions. The principles of *Babywise*—particularly the parent-directed feeding guidelines—will help you strike the right balance between the two.

Introduced in the last chapter, PDF is a proactive approach to infant care. It creates and maintains for your baby healthy patterns that enhance physical, neurological, and mental development. At the same time, PDF is flexible enough to meet the growing emotional needs of the child. This flexibility is a major difference between PDF and the extremes of psychoanalytical thought and behaviorism.

The Need for Order

Order speaks of routine and scheduling. Unfortunately, there are still some whose only understanding of an infant schedule comes from old wives' tales and bad advice. They speak of rigid feeding periods when a baby cries needlessly, waiting to be fed, while his mother hardens her heart to the baby's crying. Although that description may be an accurate reflection of parenting in the 1920s, it isn't what an infant schedule should be, nor what parent-directed feeding is all about.

The PDF plan involves more than just feeding a baby. It is a twenty-four-hour strategy designed to meet not only the baby's needs, but those of the entire family. PDF is made up of three basic activities that are repeated in a rhythmical cycle throughout the day: feeding time, waketime, and naptime. Those cycles are both *routine* and *predictable*.

Before we progress further, we need to note the difference between the terms routine and predictable. That which is routine is predictable, but that which may be predictable is not always routine. For example, Chelsea's mom follows the principles of PDF. As a result, her interaction with her baby is both predictable and routine. That is, approximately the same amount of time passes from one feeding event to the next. As we will discuss later, this is an important first step in establishing continuous nighttime sleep.

Marisa's mom is following a demand-feeding approach. As a result, her interaction is very predictable (Marisa cries and her mother responds), but it is not routine. One hour may pass between two feedings. Marisa cries; her mom feeds her again. Three hours may pass the next time, followed by two hours. Although feeding for Marisa is predictable, it is also very erratic. The erratic nature of the demand-feed (or free-feed) theory negatively impacts Marisa's metabolism.

In contrast, Chelsea's mom understands the benefits of routine, and she appreciates the accompanying sense of security. Her baby shows by her positive response to routine that she has an inner need for an outward system of structure. Although *in utero* nutrition continually passes on to the baby, there are spikes—peak periods—of nutritional consumption. Those times correlate with the mother's basic three-meals-a-day routine. Outside the womb, a basic feeding routine provides structure that encourages the natural rhythms of a child to synchronize with those of the rest of the family.

For example, infants are not born with a mature central nervous system. Regular and predictable parental interaction is needed to balance a baby's body functions until the central nervous system is mature enough to take over. By contrast, lack of regularity sends a negative signal to the baby's body, creating metabolic confusion that negatively affects his or her hunger, digestive, and sleep/wake cycles.

The importance of an infant schedule is well recognized. In most neonatal units, you will find that premature infants, twins, triplets, and low-birthweight babies, are not allowed to feed on demand but are placed on a strict three-hour feeding schedule. The reason?

Medical authorities know that when you deal with life-and-death situations, babies thrive better when fed on routine as compared to nonroutine feedings. The PDF principles reflect such conservative care.

Putting Chelsea on a *flexible* schedule benefits not only her but her mom, too. Her mother now has the confidence that comes with knowing what will happen next. Life becomes more predictable for her, for Chelsea, and for the rest of the family. She can plan her day's activities, knowing that Chelsea's needs will be met. That results in a proactive style of parenting, rather than a reactive one, which is usually less than satisfactory.

Chelsea's mom is also healthier as a result of feeding her baby on a routine. She obtains restful sleep and has time for the exercise she needs. As a breast-feeding mom, she is more likely to be successful with a daily infant plan than with random feeding periods. If Chelsea has siblings, a plan will allow her mom and dad to give them needed time as well. Everyone wins with PDF.

Marisa's mom, on the other hand, is so concerned about her baby's developing emotions that she has failed to see the importance of structure to her child. Physical structure is what helps balance Marisa's emotions. To compensate, Marisa's parents are more susceptible to every new fad or gadget coming out on the parenting market that promises to settle their baby down—everything from an electric crib rocker to a teddy bear with a mother-sounding heart beat to nightly drives in the car—all to get Marisa to sleep. There is a better way.

It's hard not to feel sorry for Marisa's parents. They have been victimized by wrong philosophies and, as a result, everyone in the family suffers. Without common sense in a parent's thinking, the most obvious solutions to basic sleep problems are no longer options.

The Advantages of PDF

The parent-directed feeding plan has many advantages. It benefits Chelsea, her mom, and her dad in a number of different ways. Here is a partial list of the benefits of this plan.

Benefits of PDF for Chelsea

1. Chelsea's metabolism is stable, since parental interaction is regular and predictable.

2. Chelsea's digestive system will have fewer problems with colic-like symptoms when compared with her demand-fed cousin.

3. Chelsea's nighttime sleep cycles will be stabilized. Between the third and eighth week, her mom can expect her to begin sleeping seven to eight hours straight through the night. Chelsea will probably sleep ten to twelve hours per night by week twelve. By that time, her cousin Marisa will still be waking twice in the middle of the night for a snack, and is apt to continue in that pattern for the next two years.

4. Chelsea doesn't have to be manipulated to sleep. When bedtime comes, Chelsea's mom and dad place her in her crib and she falls asleep. If there is any fussing, it's usually very limited. Marisa's mother, on the other hand, tries to nurse her to sleep, but the ordeal sometimes takes hours. As soon as she puts Marisa in her crib, she is likely to wake up, and her mom is forced to start the process all over again. This style of parenting grows old very quickly.

5. Chelsea's stimulus barrier—a person's ability to filter out unnecessary sounds, such as background noises—matures more quickly. Marisa tends to experience restlessness, and startles more easily at the slightest sound, both during the day and the night.

6. Chelsea moves naturally from dependence to independence. The nature of the PDF program fosters *relational* security. That is, a baby's security depends on his or her developing relationships, not on proximity to the baby's mother. In contrast, mothers who are constantly attentive by way of baby slings, shared sleep, and demand feeding, all in hopes of fostering security, too often accomplish the opposite. That statement is easily proven. Just remove the child from mom at any point and observe how secure he or she appears. It's disheartening for a parent to see her child in a state of hysteria over being confronted with a need for independence, while other children the same age are maturing appropriately in their independence.

7. Chelsea allows others to care for her because she has learned from her earliest days to receive comfort from other caregivers.

8. Chelsea is learning to be at peace with her environment. PDF fosters an environment of learning from the beginning, which enhances her learning potential. Learning disorders associated with nonstructured styles of parenting—including deficiencies in sitting, focusing, and concentrating—are minimized with routine. If you are thinking about home schooling in the future, we believe an infant routine is the starting point for optimum development.

Benefits of PDF for Chelsea's Mother

1. Chelsea's mother naturally has a rational response to mothering, since Chelsea's basic needs become predictable. Marisa's mom

tends to be "strung out" emotionally. Life is not predictable for her or her daughter.

2. Chelsea's mother is not enslaved to her child, since the program allows her to keep life's demands in balance. Marisa's mom, though, in a sense is in bondage to her daughter's unpredictability.

3. Chelsea's mother, with PDF, develops a metabolic process that naturally encourages a mother's body to synchronize with her natural rhythmic cycles. That, in turn, enhances successful breast-feeding. In contrast, the nature of demand-feeding forces Marisa's mom to provide numerous periods of snack feeding. Many moms who feed their babies on demand are so tired that they prematurely give up breast-feeding.

4. Chelsea's mom, who is breast-feeding and using PDF, rarely has problems with her let-down reflex. In contrast, Marisa's mom nurses her baby so often that sometimes her let-down is delayed, frustrating her child. Or worse yet, her let-down may not occur at all.

5. Chelsea's mother, because of her routine, tends to move back into hormonal balance sooner than non-PDF mothers. Marisa's mom had a terrible bout with postpartum depression. Her condition is not unusual for mothers whose bodies are worn out from the absence of structure.

6. Chelsea's mom not only regains her physical strength quickly, but also returns to her other roles in life—such as wife, daughter, neighbor, and friend. Marisa's mom is often not in the mood for seeing anyone.

7. Overall, Chelsea's mom and the other mothers who follow PDF have less maternal anxiety than mothers who choose to demand-feed. Much of the guesswork has been removed with the

reliable twenty-four-hour plan. Life becomes very predictable and reassuring.

Benefits of PDF for Chelsea's Father

1. Chelsea's father is involved from the beginning with more than offering an occasional bottle. PDF encourages dad to be active in assessment and decision-making. Marisa's dad is not part of the management team.

2. Chelsea's father's relationship with his wife is the cornerstone of the family. From the beginning, both of Chelsea's parents have cared for her, not just one of them.

The Benefits of Routine

In light of the short length of time we have with our children until they are grown, an infant feeding plan may not seem very significant. But it is! A plan is the first step to successful parenting. Without one, you could end up like Marisa and her mom.

Parent-directed feeding successfully addresses the rhythmical needs of your infant. The principles work because they reinforce— rather than violate—the natural laws of development. PDF is not a prepackaged program, but one you design for the benefit of all your family members. If you follow the basic principles associated with this plan, you will be ready and competent to lovingly direct the life of your child.

Questions for Review

1. What are the two popular misconceptions regarding infant schedules?

2. What is parent-directed feeding?

3. Describe the difference between Chelsea's and Marisa's nighttime sleep patterns.

4. What is "relational security"?

5. How can you easily prove the lack of security in a baby who is carried all day in a sling?

Chapter Four

Hunger and Sleep Cycles

O ne of the most obvious benefits of parent-directed feeding is the establishment of stable nighttime sleep patterns. That means your baby sleeps all night, along with the rest of the family. Healthy, full-term babies are born with the ability to sleep continuously for seven to eight hours during the night, usually within eight weeks. Much of your success will depend on your parenting philosophy and feeding practices.

Many attempts have been made to explain why some babies sleep through the night early and others don't. The theories range from simple to complex, from logical to bizarre. Speaking from inexperience, the new mother usually arrives at the simplest explanation: "Every child is different. Some can sleep, others can't." The behavioral clinician may suggest that a child's temperament is the determining influence on sleep patterns: "Some children are easier to handle by nature; some are more difficult." Others may suggest that the need of each child varies: "A high-need baby requires more nocturnal parental interaction; a low-need baby requires less." Although each statement contains a grain of truth, the statements themselves are incomplete.

The feeding pattern you establish with your little one appears to be the key to controlling nighttime sleep behavior. During feeding times, parents have the greatest interaction with their newborn. That interaction triggers a natural cause-and-effect relationship. When Chelsea's mom starts out with routine feeding periods, she is actually establishing stable hunger patterns. When these feeding patterns stabilize, nighttime sleep patterns will soon follow suit. When feeding periods are routinely inconsistent, nighttime sleep is not achieved.

Routine Feedings and Nightime Sleep

There is a direct relationship between regular daytime feeding periods and nighttime sleep patterns. Chelsea's cousin, Marisa, having been fed on demand, now has great difficulty establishing stable and uninterrupted nighttime sleep. Sometimes she wakes as often as every two hours on a recurring basis, and she may do this routinely for two years, according to some studies.[1] That pattern is not healthy for Marisa or her mom. No wonder her mother seems tired all the time.

Marisa's mom believes her daughter's lack of ability to sleep continuously through the night is a result of breast-feeding. She read somewhere that breast-fed babies are not capable of sleeping through the night. Actually, failure to establish continuous nighttime sleep is not associated with breast-feeding at all, but with demand-feeding (in other words, it's caused by lack of routine). Demand-fed babies don't sleep through the night. Chelsea and thousands of other breast-fed babies on PDF sleep through the night just fine, without damaging lactation.

Chelsea's mom realizes continuous nighttime sleep has less to do with the food offered (breast milk or formula) than it has to do with the presence or lack of routine. Mothers who demand-feed their babies with formula usually end up with the same unfortunate results experienced by moms who breast-feed on demand.

Your feeding philosophy is the starting point in establishing a routine. How a mother meets her child's nutritional needs during the day will either interact positively or negatively with lower-brain function, which regulates the baby's biological time clock. If there is no regularity to feeding, there is no basis for stable patterns—a routine—to develop. Newborns on PDF establish many restful and continuous periods of sleep. This nighttime sleep is in addition to the baby's regular naptimes during the day.

Although sleep research is still a new frontier in behavioral pediatrics, three facts stand out from our experience:

Fact 1: Healthy, full-term newborns have a predisposition for continuous nighttime sleep by the eighth week.

Fact 2: Newborn sleep cycles do not stabilize until hunger and digestive patterns are stabilized.

Fact 3: Routine parental interaction helps stabilize hunger patterns. Inconsistent parental interaction fosters irregular hunger patterns, thereby creating instability in the child's sleep/wake cycles.

When you consider these facts, especially the final one, how should you interact with your newborn in order to achieve optimum development? You need to follow a basic routine from the beginning. Who is in the best position to determine that routine—the child or the parent? Marisa's parents wrongly believe their baby should regulate her own routine, and that their job is to respond. After all, a baby knows when she is hungry and when she is ready for sleep, doesn't she?

Yes, babies know when they are hungry, but they are not capable of regulating their hunger patterns. And yes, babies know when they are tired, but they are not capable of establishing stable sleep/wake cycles on their own. Parental guidance is necessary.

Parent-directed feeding provides the necessary guidance by establishing a rhythmic structure suited for helping your baby's metabolism stabilize. A newborn needs outward structure until his central nervous system is fully developed. PDF is that outward structure. The principles of PDF work for Chelsea because they are directed toward the constant factors of her development, not the variables of her temperament. As Chelsea's mother provides daily interaction with her through predictable feeding patterns, her hunger and sleep/wake cycles stabilize.

Hunger Patterns

From the point of birth onward, infant hunger patterns will become either stable and regular or unstable and inconsistent. The determining factor is whether or not you are following a feeding routine with a minimum of two-and-a-half hours from the end of the last feeding to the beginning of the next. When infants are fed on the PDF plan, their hunger patterns stabilize. The reason for this stabilization is that the hunger mechanism (digestion and absorption) operates as if it has a metabolic memory that is reinforced by routine. If Chelsea's feeding periods are regular, she will establish a hunger metabolism that is stable and predictable. For example, if her mom feeds her at approximately 7:00 A.M., 10:00 A.M., 1:00 P.M., 4:00 P.M., 7:00 P.M., and 10:00 P.M., her baby's hunger metabolism will begin to line up to those times. But this happens only when the feeding periods are routine. As the baby's hunger metabolism stabilizes, her digestive metabolism stabilizes.

In contrast, erratic feeding periods confuse an infant's young memory. Since the parental response changes from day to day, often hour to hour, there is no chance for the hunger mechanism to stabilize. With the way Marisa is being fed, any programmed stability will be a matter of chance. That's why Marisa will probably take two years before she sleeps through the night, and why she is a candidate for sleep-related problems in childhood.

Sleep/Wake Cycles

Because Chelsea's sleep is influenced by the parent-directed feeding plan, on the other hand, she will tend to establish many more restful periods than her cousin. In the early months, an infant sleeps most of the time. Half of this sleep time is spent in quiet sleep (relaxed sleep pattern, or RSP) and the other half in active sleep (active sleep pattern, or ASP). Researchers tell us these two patterns should alternate about every thirty to forty-five minutes during sleep time.

There are noticeable differences between these two patterns. During the relaxed sleep state, you will see a more peaceful baby. The baby's face is relaxed, eyelids closed and still, and he or she has very few body movements. The baby's breathing is quiet and very regular.

The active sleep state is a more restless state. In both children and adults, this is our dream state. The extent to which infants dream is not yet known. During this period, the arms and legs stir, the eyes and mouth flutter, and facial activities—such as sucking, frowning, and chewing motions—occur. Breathing is irregular and slightly faster.

How do ASP and RSP relate to feeding patterns in the first twelve weeks? Although Marisa experiences some RSP, she fails to experience the cycle on a continual basis. From the start, she has been put to the breast ten to fifteen times a day and allowed to suckle for forty-five minutes to an hour. With that type of feeding pattern, there isn't much time left for the RSP cycle to repeat itself, so she experiences less of the deeper, quiet sleep. Marisa's nights are much like her days—a series of naps between feedings.

On the other hand, Chelsea experiences the necessary length of sleep between feedings, enabling the RSP/ASP cycle to naturally repeat itself. And she experiences that sleep routinely.

Is Infant Sleep Deprivation Dangerous?

Imagine what would happen to an adult who was not allowed to sleep more than three hours at a stretch for one week. The negative effects to his or her mature central nervous system are well established. He or she will become irritable, weak, will find it difficult to concentrate, may experience partial neurologic shutdown, and so on. But what about an infant whose central nervous system is still developing? Our question then is: To what extent does sleep deprivation negatively impact an infant's developing central nervous system?

Imagine parenting in such a way that your baby is not allowed to sleep continuously for eight hours, even one night out of three hundred and sixty-five. Couldn't many of the learning disabilities associated with a nonstructured approach to parenting be rooted in something as basic as the absence of continuous nights of sleep in the first year of life, when the higher brain is still developing? We think this is certainly a possibility.

Sleep Props Hinder Continuous Nighttime Sleep

Where there is the ability, there is the capacity. The typical infant has both the natural ability and the capacity to sleep through the night sometime within the first two months of life. It is an acquired skill that is enhanced by routine.

Sleep deprivation in infants and toddlers has much less to do with *nature* than with *nurture*. Sleep is a natural function of the body. The primary cue for infant sleep is sleepiness. Sleep cues are influenced (often negatively) by a variety of sleep association props. Some sleep props, such as a special blanket or a stuffed animal, are harmless, while others are addictive. For some parents, the problem is getting the child to fall asleep initially. For others, the challenge is getting the child to fall back to sleep without a prop, once prematurely awakened. The three most common negative sleep props are:

1. Intentionally nursing a baby to sleep.
2. Rocking a baby to sleep.
3. Sleeping with your baby (shared sleep).

Let's take a look at each of these potentially harmful sleep-inducing techniques.

Intentionally Nursing Your Baby to Sleep

Is nursing your baby to sleep an appropriate method of sleep control? We believe the answer is *no*. Such sleep cues only create an unnecessary sleep dependency.

The scenario is all too familiar. A mother nurses her baby to sleep. Slowly lifting herself from the chair, she begins moving toward the crib. Holding her breath, she gently puts the baby down. Then, frozen for a moment, she anxiously waits for peace to settle over the crib. She backs up to the door, hoping to make her escape. If the baby fusses, the process begins all over again.

Parents don't need to be in bondage to their baby's sleep needs. A routine allows infants to establish healthy sleep patterns and to be put down in the crib *awake*.

Rocking Your Baby to Sleep

The issue is not whether you should rock or cuddle your baby. We trust that happens regularly. But are you creating sleep props that interfere with your child's ability to fall asleep initially or to fall back asleep when prematurely awakened?

Similar to rocking a baby to sleep are modern mechanical sleep props—such as the clothes dryer. (Yes, the clothes dryer!) Someone discovered that if a baby is placed on top of an operating dryer, the dryer may create enough vibration to lull the baby to sleep. This is not a safe or wise practice. Another method is the naptime or nighttime car ride. In this scenario, the sound of the motor and the vibrating chassis of the car sends the baby to sleep land. Both approaches sometimes work—temporarily. That is, they work until the dryer runs out of time, the car runs out of gas, or you run out of patience.

Sleeping with Your Baby

The most serious security-related sleep problems we have witnessed are those associated with parents who sleep with their babies. Sharing sleep with children puts them at risk both physically and emotionally. Physically, rolling on top of the child and smothering him to death is a real threat.[2] Such infant deaths are labeled "parental overlay," and are just now receiving the media attention they deserve.

Emotionally, this method is passively abusive. It can create a state of abnormal dependency on the sleep prop to the point that the child actually fears falling asleep when transitioned to his own bed. As the child moves into toddlerhood, he expresses that fear through the need for his parent to lie down with him at naptime until he falls asleep. In several of our recovery cases, toddlers used vomiting to get the attention of a parent. Others rhythmically bang their head against the wall. Shared sleep creates a false sense of security. Too often, children can't function outside the parent's presence, since their security is based on proximity, not relationship.

We believe sleeping with your baby in the long run creates needs instead of preventing or meeting them. The real question is: Why use sleep association props in the first place, when a basic routine will naturally enhance restful sleep? If you put your baby to bed awake, she will establish longer and stronger sleep cycles than if you put her down already asleep. None of the sleep manipulation methods listed above offers any healthy advantages. You must think of the long-term effects. Don't create a behavior that will later call for retraining. Feed your baby, rock her and love her, but put her down before she falls asleep. (See Chapter 10 for an expanded discussion on the "family bed" theory.)

Questions for Review

1. Explain how feeding patterns influence nighttime sleep behavior.

2. What are three facts that relate to infant sleep?

    a.

    b.

    c.

3. Should you allow your baby to regulate his or her own routine? Explain your answer.

4. How do erratic feeding periods confuse an infant's young memory?

5. What is a "sleep prop"?

6. List three negative sleep props which hinder nighttime sleep.

   a.

   b.

   c.

Chapter Five

Facts on Feeding

ow you feed your baby is perhaps the most basic task of infant management. Since a baby's sucking and rooting reflexes are well developed at birth, he will satisfy those reflexes by rooting and sucking on anything near his mouth. Whether feeding is accomplished by a bottle or the breast is not as important as the gentle and tender cuddling you give him during feeding.

Your decision to bottle- or breast-feed must be free of any coercion or manipulation. You will make the right decision when you are best informed. There is no question that breast-feeding is preferred for its physiological benefits. A mother's milk is a complete and perfect food. It is easily digested, provides excellent nutrition, and contains the right balance of proteins and fats. It also provides additional antibodies that are necessary for establishing your baby's early immune system.[1]

Breast-feeding has advantages for mom, as well. It helps speed the return of her uterus to its normal size and shape. It is also the most economical and convenient way to feed her baby. There is no cleanup, storing, or heating needed, and there is nothing to pack away when you travel. While stored in the breast, the milk never spoils or gets too old to use.

Transforming a woman into a good mother is one thing breast-feeding can't promise to do. There is no "good mother" hormone, and much more is required than just bringing a baby to breast. We believe strongly in breast-feeding, but don't believe in breast-feeding at all costs. What do we mean by that? Although breast milk is a significant link to the physical well being of a baby, the act of breast-feeding itself is not the genesis of psychological health. It is not a silver bullet assuring a love attachment or security. What *is* critical to optimal development, is the presence of routine in one's parenting. It isn't the importance of breast-feeding that is in question, then, but which *method* of breast-feeding (demand-feeding versus PDF) best complements the overall advancement of the child in all critical areas of development—should you choose to breast-feed your baby.

In Chapter 3, we compared the developmental success of the two approaches as they relate to early training of infants, pretoddlers, and toddlers. We examined the results of these feeding methods in the areas of taking naps; continuous nighttime sleep; fussiness versus contentment; signs of insecurity; family attachment as compared to mother attachment; the percentages of "high-need" babies in each case; sitting, focusing, and concentrating skills; self-play adeptness; problem-solving skills; the baby's ability to yield to parental direction; learning disability tendencies; and other matters basic to the first two years of life. Since success in all those areas is more important to us than the single category of lactation, and since there is more to good parenting than successful lactation, we don't believe breast-feeding must be accomplished at the expense of other vital aspects of development. There may come a time when going to the bottle, rather than some breast-feeding extreme, is the most loving thing a mother can do for her baby. Both bottle- and breast-feeding provide opportunities to cuddle, care, and love. (Bottle-feeding and formula are discussed in more detail later in this chapter.)

Milk Production

If breast-feeding is your choice, there are a few basic principles you need to understand. Most important is that breast-feeding success is based on demand and supply. The supply of milk produced by the glands is proportional to the demand placed on the system—the greater the demand, the greater the supply.

Marisa's mother was told her milk production was directly related to the number of feedings she offered—the more feedings, the greater the milk production. While there is some truth in this, the statement as a whole is not accurate. Certainly a mother who takes her baby to breast five times a day will produce more milk than the one who offers only one feeding. However, there are limits. A mother who takes her baby to her breast twelve, fifteen, or twenty times a day will not produce any more milk than the mom who takes her baby to breast six to seven times a day.

The difference between the two moms is *qualitative* feeding versus *quantitative* feeding. With qualitative feeding, you eliminate the need for continual snacking. And that is exactly what many feedings become—a snack, not a meal. The opinion that many feedings automatically equate to maximized milk production is a common misunderstanding. We counsel many mothers who do poorly with milk production as a result of unlimited feedings. Successful breast-feeding includes more factors than just bringing the baby to the breast frequently.

Part of a mother's ability to produce milk is tied to the demand placed on her system. Two factors associated with the demand side of breast-milk production are: 1) the need for appropriate *stimulation* at each feeding, and 2) the correct amount of *time* between feedings. Without proper stimulation, no matter how many times an infant goes to the breast, milk production will be limited. Too many snack feedings (with too little time between feedings) may reduce proper stimulation; too few feedings (too much time between feedings) reduces milk production. Time and stimulation are interrelated, and both are necessary for successful breast-feeding.

When we speak of breast stimulation, we are referring to the intensity of the suck. The hunger drive is a consistent influence on the sucking reflex. This drive is associated with the time it takes for an infant to digest and absorb the milk. The infant who is fed on a basic three-hour routine and whose digestive metabolism is stabilized, will demand more milk, thereby stimulating greater milk production as compared to the child who feeds more often but demands less. Again, the issue is hunger feeding versus snack feeding.

For example, the newborn who feeds every one-and-a-half hours will stimulate only enough milk production to meet that need. That's why demand-fed babies feed more often—they snack more often. They are not getting a complete meal, but a partial one. That may also be the reason so many new mothers get discouraged and give up breast-feeding so quickly; feeding is practically all they do, around the clock.

On the other hand, an infant nursing every three hours will signal for greater milk production. Since the need is greater, the supply is increased. Because the supply is increased, the baby goes longer between feedings.

As a general guide, during the first two months you will feed your baby approximately every three hours. Sometimes it may be less and sometimes slightly more. But three hours is a healthy average. In actual practice, a three hour routine means you will nurse your baby two and one-half hours from the end of the last feeding to the start of the next. When you add twenty to thirty minutes for the actual feeding time, you will have completed a three hour cycle. Our warning is this: consistently feeding sooner than two and one-half hours can wear Mom down, causing a decrease in milk production. The word *consistently* in the above sentence is operative. There will be times when feedings will come sooner than two and one-half hours—but that is not the norm for the day. We'll discuss this further in Chapter 7, *"Establishing Your Baby's Routine."* At the other extreme, waiting more than three and one-half hours to offer a feeding can fail to produce sufficient stimulation needed for a sufficient quantity of milk. Therefore, do not rely upon the baby's cry to determine feeding. Some babies may not give you a hunger cry cue.

The Let-Down Reflex

When a baby begins to suckle on his mother's breast, a message is sent to the mother's pituitary gland, which in turn releases several hormones. The hormone prolactin is necessary for milk production, and the hormone oxytocin is required for milk release. The most important factor in the continued release of prolactin is proper nipple stimulation. Without this stimulation, milk will not be produced, no matter how many times an infant goes to the breast. A continuous routine will help maximize milk production.

Oxytocin causes the cells around the milk glands to contract, forcing milk into the ducts. When that happens, it's said that the milk has been *let down*. Some mothers experience a tingling or pressure sensation at the point of let-down. Without this reflex, the milk would stay in the glands. The most reliable sign of a let-down is your baby's rhythmic swallowing of milk.

The milk that is released is called the *hindmilk*, or mature milk. This high-protein and high-fat-content milk is rich in calories (thirty to forty per ounce). Before the milk is let down, your baby will receive a milk substance stored in the ducts under the areola (the flesh encircling the nipples). This *foremilk*, as it is called, is more diluted and limited in nutritional value.

Mothers following PDF have little or no problem with the let-down reflex, compared to those who demand-feed. There are two reasons for this. First, routine plays an important part in proper let-down. Not only does the mind need a routine to maintain order and efficiency, but the body does as well. The very nature of inconsistent feeding wears on a woman's body.

A second reason is the high confidence level of the mother who follows a routine. For her, there is no need to question or second guess what will happen next. She is confident, and her confidence aids the successful working of her let-down reflex. In fact, because of her routine she is much more in tune with her baby and the baby's needs. She knows intuitively when something is wrong because it falls so obviously outside the normal pattern of her baby's behavior. In

contrast, the lack of confidence that comes with the absence of routine only produces worrisome fear and anxiety (fear in not knowing
if the baby received enough at the last feeding, anxiety in not knowing what to do next). There is no "normal" for these mothers. That's
what further perpetuates the anxiety cycle. Such anxiety can impact
a mother to the extent that she does not let down her milk at all.

Breast Milk and Baby's Digestion

Does an empty stomach trigger the hunger drive? No. Proper
digestion and absorption of food does. The purpose of digestion is to
break down the various food groups into proteins, fats, and carbohydrates. The end product of digestion is absorption. Absorption,
which takes place primarily in the small intestine, is the process by
which the broken-down food molecules pass through the intestinal
lining into the bloodstream. As absorption is accomplished, the
blood-sugar level drops. That drop, in turn, sends a signal to the
hypothalamus gland calling for more food. A drop in blood-sugar,
not an empty stomach, is the signal for more food.

Breast milk is digested faster than formula, but that fact doesn't
justify unlimited feedings. Rather than comparing breast milk to formula, it's more useful to look at the amount of breast milk consumed
at each feeding. Demand-fed babies tend to snack all day. PDF babies
have a complete meal at each feeding. The child who nurses frequently and takes in fewer ounces of milk will naturally be hungry
more often. In contrast, the child on PDF takes in more ounces of
milk at a feeding, thereby causing the digestive and absorption
processes to take longer.

Nursing Your Baby

During the first few days of nursing, find a comfortable position in which to nurse, possibly using a pillow under your supporting arm to lessen the stress on your neck and upper back. Correct positioning of the baby is critical for successful lactation.

Proper Positioning

Let's suppose you have a newborn daughter. When the baby nurses, she should take both the nipple and all or much of the areola into her mouth. Encourage the baby to latch on to the areola. With correct positioning, your baby's entire body is facing you (head, chest, stomach, and legs). She will not latch on correctly if her head is facing you but the rest of her body isn't. With your nipple, stroke lightly downward on your baby's lower lip until she opens her mouth. Be careful not to touch her upper lip. When her mouth opens wide, center your nipple and pull her close to you, so that the tip of her nose is touching your breast and her knees are touching your abdomen. When the baby is correctly latched on, nursing will not be painful. Successful latching is made difficult if the baby's head is toward the breast but the body is allowed to turn away from the mother. If there is discomfort, remove her and relatch her.

A nursing baby often has a remarkably strong suck. If you try to pull the nipple away, she will just suckle harder. To remove her without hurting yourself, slip your little finger between the corner of her mouth and your breast. That will break the suction, allowing you to take her off easily.

The Nursing Periods

Current wisdom governing the length of nursing periods for the first few days is still being debated. The advice is as varied as individual experience. We suggest the following:

The Very First Nursing Period. If possible, nurse your baby soon after birth (within the first hour-and-a-half), since that is when newborns are usually most alert. We suggest you strive for fifteen minutes per side (a minimum of ten minutes per side), remembering the importance of positioning the baby properly on the breast. If your baby wants to nurse longer during this first feeding, allow him or her to do so. In fact, with the first several feedings you can go as long as the two of you are comfortable. Both breasts need to be stimulated at each feeding, and the initial time frame mentioned above will allow for sufficient breast stimulation.

The First Five Days. Over the course of the next three to five days, maintain your basic two-and-a-half- to three-hour routine, nursing fifteen to twenty minutes per side. That means your average nursing period falls between thirty and forty minutes per feeding during this first week. Some mothers nurse fifteen to twenty minutes from each side, burping their baby before switching breasts. Other mothers find it helpful to employ a ten-ten-five-five method. They alternate each breast after ten minutes (burping the baby between sides), and then offer each breast for five additional minutes. This second method is especially helpful when you have a sleepy baby, helping to assure that both breasts are stimulated. Please note that these figures are *goals* based on averages. Some newborns nurse faster and more efficiently, others nurse efficiently but slightly slower. If your baby wants to nurse longer let him do so.

After Your Milk Comes In. Once your milk is in, your nursing periods will average fifteen minutes per side. As just mentioned, some babies nurse faster, some slower. Studies show that in established lactation, a baby can empty the breasts in seven to ten minutes per side, providing he or she is sucking vigorously. By pointing out that fact, we are not encouraging less time at the breast but showing just how much can be accomplished in a short amount of time.

Under normal circumstances, your baby will take what he or she needs within thirty minutes. The belief that nonnutritive sucking beyond the thirty minutes enhances a baby's security or heightens a baby's sense of love, is an interesting idea that lacks serious scientific support. Security and love result from the overall parent-child relationship, not one isolated factor. If you feel your baby has a need for nonnutritive sucking, a pacifier can meet the need without compromising your routine.

Don't be discouraged if your baby doesn't catch on right away; the baby won't starve. Your infant is born with sufficient water and extra calories to sustain him or her until your milk comes in, usually between three and six days. During that period, some weight loss in the baby is normal and expected. (Note: Guidelines for monitoring your baby's nutritional intake are listed in Chapter 6. Please study our recommendations carefully.) By twelve to fourteen days, your baby should have regained his or her birth weight. *It is important that you learn to listen to how well your baby swallows. That signal, as well as five to seven wet diapers per day, are good indicators that your baby is getting enough milk for healthy growth.*

The first milk produced is a thick, yellowish liquid called *colostrum.* Colostrum is high in protein (at least five times as high as mature milk) and has less fat and sugar than later milk. It is a protein concentrate that takes longer to digest and is rich in antibodies. Some mothers experience tenderness in the first few days before their milk comes in. This is due to the thickness of the colostrum and to the infant sucking especially hard to remove it. The baby's pattern is suck, suck, suck, then swallow. Once your milk comes in, your baby responds with a rhythmic suck, swallow, suck, swallow, suck, swallow, suck, swallow. At that point, the hard sucking is reduced and the tenderness goes away.

Nursing twins is addressed on page 171 and jaundice in newborns is on page 170.

Breast Versus Bottle

We know the nutritional and health-benefit disparity between breast milk and formula over the first twelve weeks of your baby's life is substantial. By six months of age, the disparity is also great, but not to the same extent as the first twelve weeks. (Breast-feeding for six months is the minimum duration recommended by the American Academy of Pediatrics.) Between six and nine months, the difference between what is best and what is good continues to narrow. That is partly due to the fact that other food sources are now part of your baby's diet. Between nine and twelve months, the nutritional value of breast milk drops and food supplements are usually needed. Nursing beyond a year in our society is done more out of preference than for an absolute nutritional need.

Mother's milk is clearly superior to formula. But what about when it comes to nurturing? Which is best, breast or bottle? In times past, writers stressed the value of breast-feeding and labeled bottle-feeding as a way of rejecting a child and as a sign that the mother lacks warmth. Some have said she is renouncing her biological role as a woman and her emotional role as a mother. Others considered bottle-fed children to have less of an advantage in life than those who are breast-fed. Actually, studies over the last sixty years that have attempted to correlate the method of infant feeding with emotional development in later life have failed to support any of these conclusions. A mother's attitude toward her child as expressed in the total context of parenting is more important than any one isolated factor, such as the manner of feeding.

Bottle Feeding

Bottle-feeding is not a twentieth-century discovery, but a practice that has been around thousands of years. Our ancestors made bottles out of wood, porcelain, pewter, glass, copper, leather, and cow horns. Historically, unprocessed animal's milk was the principal nourishment used with bottle-feeding. But because the milk was easily contaminated, infant mortality was high.

When bottle-feeding was in fashion during the first half of this century, one size fit all. But today your grocer's shelves are filled with options. Besides the standard glass and plastic bottles, there are those with disposable bags, designer styles, handles, and even animal shapes. All of these choices come in a vast array of colors and prints.

To add to a mother's confusion is the selection of the proper nipple. You can find anything from a nursing nipple that is most like mom, to an orthodontic nipple. There are juice, formula, water, and even cereal nipples. Actually, the most important consideration is to make sure you purchase a nipple that has the right-sized hole. Too large a hole causes the child to drink too fast. Excessive spitting up and projectile vomiting can be signs of too-rapid fluid intake. A hole that is too small creates a hungry and discontented child. These simple tips will prevent what may seem to be major feeding problems with your baby.[2]

An advantage to bottle-feeding is that it allows others to participate. Feeding time for dad is just as special to him as it is to mom, and fathers should not be denied the opportunity to participate. The same is true with grandparents, brothers, and sisters. Raising children is a family affair. You should try to keep it that way.

Formula

If bottle-feeding is your choice, take the time to sit down and hold your baby during feeding times. You need the rest and your baby needs the cuddling. Also, holding your baby will help prevent your child from becoming attached to the bottle, since he alone will not be in control of his eating.

As a general rule, you should not feed your baby while he or she is lying completely flat, such as when the mother is nursing in the lying-down position. It is thought that swallowing while lying down may allow fluid to enter the middle ear, leading to ear infections. Avoid propping up the bottle for the same reasons. We also caution mothers not to put an older child (six months and up) to bed with a bottle. This is true not only for health factors relating to ear infections but also for oral hygiene. When a child falls asleep with a bottle in his mouth, the sugar in the formula that remains in the mouth coats the teeth, causing tooth decay.

The most important decision you will make about bottle-feeding is what to put inside the bottle. Some of the choices will be made for you, either by the hospital in which you deliver or by your pediatrician. If either you or your husband have a history of milk allergies, mention it to your doctor. That may influence the type of formula the pediatrician recommends.

Formulas these days have properties closely matched to those of breast milk, including the proper balance and quantity of proteins, fats, and carbohydrates. Cow's milk and baby formula are not the same. Formula is designed for a baby's digestive system; cow's milk is not, and should not be given to a child less than a year old. Check with your pediatrician or your hospital for more information regarding the different manufacturers of formula.

The amount of formula taken at each feeding will vary with the baby's age. The average, as with breast-fed babies, is anywhere from one-and-a-half to three ounces per feeding in the first several weeks, with a gradual increase as the child grows. If you prepare a four-ounce bottle for each feeding and allow your baby to take as much as he or she wants, the baby will tend to stop when full. Keep in mind that a larger baby might take more milk, but not necessarily. As with breast-fed babies, the feeding routine is what establishes the corresponding hunger patterns, and not the substance or the amount of food.

Formula-fed babies need to be burped after every one-half ounce at first. By the time your baby is between four and six months old, he or she will probably be able to take the full six to eight ounces before burping. With both breast-feeding and bottle-feeding, there is a certain amount of spitting up that takes place. When that happens, don't be alarmed. However, if you find your infant rejecting all his food frequently, contact your pediatrician.

Breast milk is the best form of infant nourishment. But if you choose not to nurse, or can't nurse, or if you decide to discontinue nursing within the first twelve months, that in no way reflects badly upon you as a mother. Just as breast-feeding doesn't make you a good mother, bottle-feeding doesn't make you a bad one.

Burping Your Baby

There are several satisfactory methods of burping your baby. We want to share a few basic techniques with you. The baby that has been properly burped is a much happier baby—about that you will have no doubt!

1. Place the palm of your hand over the baby's stomach, hook your thumb around the side of your baby, and wrap the rest of your fingers around the chest area. Your hand should be the only support for the baby. You may rest the baby's bottom on your knee, but allow all of the baby's weight to be placed on your supporting hand. Lean the baby over your hand. If the baby is wiggling or needs further support, you may hold his or her hands in your supporting hand. Cup your hand and pat the baby's back. (See figure 5.1.) Note:

Figure 5.1

77

Whenever you pat your baby's back as described here, do so firmly, but avoid using too much force.

2. Place your baby high upon your shoulder so that your shoulder is placing direct pressure on the baby's stomach. Allow the baby's head and arms to freely dangle over your shoulder. Remember to hold on tightly to one leg so your baby doesn't wiggle away from you. Pat the baby's back firmly. (See Figure 5.2.)

Figure 5.2

3. In a sitting position, place your baby's legs between your legs and drape the baby over your thigh. Support the baby's head in your hands. Bring your knees together for support and pat the baby's back firmly. (See Figure 5.3.)

4. Cradle the baby in your arm with his or her bottom in your hands. (The baby's head will be resting at your elbow.) Wrap one arm and leg around your arm. Make sure the baby is facing away from you. This position allows one hand to be free at all times. (See Figure 5.4.)

Note: At times, air will become trapped in the intestines of your baby. Most babies don't like to expel gas. They will tighten their bottoms and resist the normal expulsion of gas. This can make them very uncomfortable. One way to assist your baby in the release of gas is to place him or her in a knee-chest position. Place your baby's back next to your

Figure 5.3

chest and pull his or her knees up to the chest. This position will help to alleviate your baby's discomfort.

The subject of spitting up is discussed on page 174.

Figure 5.4

Questions for Review

1. What is the difference between qualitative and quantitative feedings?

2. What two factors influence breast-milk production? Explain your answer.

3. Latching-on problems are commonly the result of what? Explain.

4. How long should you nurse your baby the first day, the first week, and after your milk comes in?

5. List two good indicators that your baby is getting enough milk for healthy growth.

    a.

    b.

6. True or False: There is a relationship between the method of infant feeding (breast-feeding versus bottle-feeding) and later personality development.

7. How often should a formula-fed baby be burped?

Chapter Six

Monitoring Your Baby's Growth

One of the many advantages of parent-directed feeding is the success mothers have with breast-feeding. Having the knowledge that her baby's nutritional needs will be met in an orderly fashion is freeing to any woman. Under the PDF plan, there is no need for guesswork. But there is a need for caution.

Being on a routine doesn't eliminate the possibility of lactation problems. Those problems don't stem from a two-and-a-half- to three-hour routine but from the variables influencing your routine and attempts to breast-feed. Those variables include the amount of sleep the mother receives; her diet, nutrition, state of mind, and age; whether this is her first child or her sixth; her desire and physical capacity to breast-feed; her nursing techniques; and the baby's ability to properly latch on. In this chapter we will survey some basic precautions for breast-feeding mothers that will help ensure healthy growth and development for their babies.

Signs of Adequate Nutrition

If you're breast-feeding, how do you know your baby is getting enough food for proper growth? There are a number of objective indicators to healthy growth and proper nutrition that you need to be aware of. Using these indicators, *monitor your baby's growth to be certain of adequate nutrition;* we can't overstate the importance of doing this.

The following are indicators of healthy growth:

1. Your baby has five to seven wet diapers a day (some saturated).
2. Your baby's urine is clear (not yellow).
3. Your baby has a strong suck and you can hear an audible swallow when the baby is nursing.
4. Your baby is alert and responsive during waketime.
5. Your baby is sleeping between feedings.
6. Your baby is gaining weight or growing in length.

These are the *unhealthy* growth indicators you need to be alert for:

1. Your baby doesn't have five to seven wet diapers a day, and none is saturated.
2. Your baby's urine is concentrated, as indicated by a bright yellow color.
3. Your baby's suck is weak and you can't hear his or her swallow during nursing.
4. Your baby is sluggish and/or slow to respond to stimulation.
5. Your baby doesn't sleep between feedings or is acting hungry all of the time.
6. Your baby is not gaining weight or growing in length.

Parents are responsible for seeing that their baby's health and nutrition needs are recognized and met. For your peace of mind, and for your baby's health, we recommend you monitor and record his or her growth with the aide of our growth chart (see Chart 6.1, "Healthy Baby Growth Chart"). This chart monitors four of the above indicators: *1) Wet diapers, 2) urine types, 3) audible swallow, and 4) hunger which occurs shortly after a feeding.*

This represents a healthy norm: Each day your baby should have five to seven wet diapers, some saturated. Diapers should indicate clear urine and not yellow, concentrated urine. At every feeding you should hear your baby swallow, and your baby should not be acting hungry soon after his or her feeding. *Any two consecutive days of deviation from what is described here as normal should be reported to your pediatrician immediately.*

Using a chart to keep track of your baby's vital health indicators can make the difference between a healthy and a sick baby. Copy the sample growth chart or make up one of your own, and post it in a convenient location (on the refrigerator, above the crib, etc.). After your milk comes in, usually at or around day three through five, monitor your baby's growth every day and record the results according to the following timetable:

Weeks one through three: record the results every day;

Weeks four through six: record the results every other day;

Weeks seven through twelve: record the results every third day;

Weeks thirteen and beyond: spot check periodically.

*Any deviation from the norm during these weeks requires a next-day observation.

CHART 6.1

Healthy Baby Growth Chart

GROWTH INDICATOR	SUMMARY OF EACH DAY						
	MON	TUES	WED	THURS	FRI	SAT	SUN
Number of wet diapers with clear urine. (normal: 5-7 per day)							
Number of wet diapers with yellow, concentrated urine. (normal: 0 per day)							
Number of feedings that audible swallow is heard. (normal: all feedings)							
Number of feedings that my baby is acting hungry after. (normal: 0 per day)							

WEEK OF_____THROUGH_____

OTHER OBSERVATIONS: _____
_____
_____

ANY TWO CONSECUTIVE DAYS OF DEVIATION FROM WHAT IS LISTED AS NORMAL SHOULD BE REPORTED TO YOUR PEDIATRICIAN IMMEDIATELY.

Weight-Gain Concerns

With the conservative practice of PDF, weight gain will be steady and continuous. We routinely monitor the progress of PDF babies and continue to find wonderful results. In our most recent survey, we randomly examined the charts of thirty babies—twenty-eight breast-fed and two bottle-fed. Length and weight gains were measured at one, four, eight, and sixteen weeks. All babies were sleeping through the night by week eight.

When compared against national pediatric norms, on average the girls fell into the 72% range for length, with continuous growth, and 54% in weight. Of the sixteen boys surveyed, their length was recorded at 61% of the national average and weight at 56%, with continuous growth. Among the boys, the average birthweight registered at 44% of the national norms. By the fourth month their weight gain on PDF placed them at 63% of the norms. This does not represent a scientific study, but it does reflect what we know to be true of PDF babies: A basic routine does not detract from proper weight gain.

Low-birthweight babies do well on a conservative routine. Although some newborns start off at the low end of the national norms, they continue to gain weight in proportion to the genetic potential for stature inherited from their parents. That is, smaller parents usually give birth to smaller babies, thus weight gain will usually be proportionately less. Add the weight-gain benefits to sleeping through the night, and the greater benefits of PDF are obvious.

Normal Weight-Gain Guide

Birth to Two Weeks:
Approximate average: Regain birthweight.

Two Weeks to Three Months:
Approximate average: Two pounds per month or one ounce per day.

Four to Six Months:
Approximate average: One pound per month or one-half ounce per day. (Doubles his or her birthweight by six months.)

One Year:
Approximate average: Two-and-a-half to three times his or her birthweight.

Babies Who Fail to Thrive

There is a difference between slow weight gain and a *failure to thrive.* With the first, weight gain is slow but consistent. "Failure to thrive" describes an infant who continues to lose weight after ten days of life, does not regain his or her birthweight by three weeks of age, or gains at an unusually slow rate beyond the first month. It's estimated that in the United States, more than two hundred thousand babies a year experience failure to thrive. The cause can be attributed to either mother or child.

Mother-Related Causes

Here are some mother-related matters that can contribute to slow or no weight gain.

1. Improper nursing technique. Many women fail at breast-feeding because the baby is not positioned properly on the breast. As

a result, he or she latches on only to the nipple and not to all or much of the areola. The end result is a hungry baby.

2. Nature or lifestyle. Insufficient milk production can be a result of nature (insufficient glandular tissue or hormones) or a mother's lifestyle (not getting enough rest or liquids). The mother simply doesn't produce enough milk, or in some cases, milk of high enough quality. If you suspect this is the case, try: a) using a breast pump to see if anything comes out; and b) discovering if your baby will take any formula after he or she has been at your breast for the proper amount of time. Report your findings to your pediatrician.

3. Poor release of milk. This indicates a problem with the mother's let-down reflex.

4. Feeding too frequently. There is an irony here, because one would think that many feedings would ensure adequate weight gain. Not necessarily! In some cases a mother can be worn out by too many ineffective feedings. When we first met Jeffrey, he was six weeks old and had gained only one pound. His mom offered him the breast each time he cried, approximately every one to one-and-a-half hours. The baby was properly latched on. Jeffrey's mother simply was fatigued. Although he was failing to thrive, the only counsel this mother received was to feed more often and to carry her baby in a sling. In contrast, we put her on a three-hour routine. Her poor health necessitated a formula supplement. In a few days, the starving child started to gain weight. In a week, he was sleeping through the night. Jeffrey's mother successfully breast-fed his subsequent siblings on the PDF plan without a weight-gain problem.

5. Feeding too infrequently. This problem can be attributed to both hyperscheduling or demand-feeding. The mother who insists on watching the clock to the minute lacks confidence in decision-

making. The clock is in control, not the parent. The hyperschedulist insists on a strict schedule, often nursing her baby no more often than every four hours. Enslavement to the clock is almost as great an evil as a mother who is in bondage to thoughtless emotions.

Some demand-fed babies request food too infrequently. As a result, the mother's breast is not sufficiently stimulated for adequate milk production. Routine feedings with a time limitation between feedings eliminates this problem. That's why neonatal and intensive care units stay close to a three-hour feeding schedule. It's healthy.

6. Not Monitoring Growth Signs. Many moms simply fail to notice their baby's healthy and unhealthy growth indicators. The Healthy Baby Growth Chart will assist you with that vital task.

Infant-Related Causes

There are several infant causes for slow or no weight gain.

1. Weak sucking. In this case, the child doesn't have the coordination or the strength to suck properly, remain latched on, or to activate the let-down reflex. As a result, the baby receives the low-calorie foremilk but not the high-calorie hindmilk.

2. Improper sucking. This can result from a number of different conditions:

a. *Tongue thrusting.* When going to breast, sometimes a baby thrusts his or her tongue forward and pushes the nipple out of his or her mouth.

b. *Tongue tied.* Latching on is made difficult when the *frenulum* (the tissue that attaches the tongue to the floor of the mouth) is too short or is attached too close to the front of the tongue.

c. *Protruding tongue*. This condition is described as the tongue forming a hump in the mouth, interfering with successful latching on.

d. *Tongue sucking*. The infant suckles on his own tongue.

3. An underlying medical problem. A weak or laborious suck (for example, one in which the child tires to the point of giving up after a few minutes of nursing) can be a symptom of cardiac or neurological failing. *If you suspect this may be the case, don't wait for your baby's next scheduled checkup. Call your pediatrician immediately.*

There are many variables involved in successful breast-milk production, but fortunately, your baby's routine is a positive one.

NOTE: Breast-feeding proficiency is usually a matter of standard review in childbirth classes. For additional help, consider taking a breast-feeding class at your local hospital or renting a "how to" video. You can attend a class and learn proper techniques of breast-feeding without accepting the instructor's personal parenting philosophies that sometimes accompany such classes. If you are concerned about your progress after your baby arrives, ask your pediatrician to observe your nursing techniques or to recommend a lactation educator or consultant.

Insufficient Milk Production

Regardless of which feeding philosophy you follow, you cannot add to what nature has left out. The anxiety created by the fear of failure is itself a contributor to milk deficiency. Because so much guilt is placed on mothers who are not successful at breast-feeding, many of them go to extremes to become milk-sufficient.

In most cultures, five percent of nursing mothers during peacetime and up to ten percent during wartime, will not produce enough milk to satisfy their infants' needs. Some mothers may initially be milk-sufficient but become insufficient by the third month. That could happen to a mother even though her baby is cooperative and sucking frequently, and she herself is using correct nursing techniques and is receiving adequate food, rest, and support from her husband and family.

Unfortunately, in our society's rush to get back to nature, there are groups who inadvertently created a perfect-mother stereotype—a "marsupial super mom"—who endlessly carries her infant, has twelve free hours a day to nurse, and who possesses an endless supply of milk. That distorted image of motherhood only creates a stigma of negligence when a mother fails to measure up to the myth that if you don't get an "A" in breast-feeding, you get an "F" in mothering.

How cruel to parade that notion before the five percent of mothers who do their best, but for reasons out of their control, are not milk-sufficient. A woman's ability to lactate, and the length of her lactation, are not valid measurements of good mothering.

Some mothers find their womanly identity in the act of breast-feeding. In practice, the relationship between the mother's breast and the child is elevated above the relationship between the mother and her child. For these women, there is an inordinate preoccupation with breast-feeding—anytime, anywhere, for any reason. In such cases, the mother may become dependent on breast-feeding to maintain her identity. There is more to nurturing a baby than responding with the breast to his or her every cry.

If You Question Your Milk Supply

If at anytime you question the adequacy of your milk supply, or observe routine fussiness after every feeding, or your baby is having difficulty going the appropriate duration between feedings, review the external stresses in your life and try to eliminate what you can. This is true whether your baby is four weeks or four months old. Are you too busy or not getting enough sleep? Are you drinking enough liquids? Is your intake of calories adequate? Are you dieting too soon? Are you following your doctor's recommendation for supplemental vitamins during lactation? Are you consuming too many dairy products? Also consider the technical aspects associated with feeding. Is the baby positioned properly and latched on correctly? If you find your baby is still not content after checking all those external factors, consider the following:

1. If You Question Your Milk Supply in the First Two Months. For a baby between three and eight weeks old, consider feeding on a strict $2\frac{1}{2}$ hour routine for five to seven days. If your milk production increases (as demonstrated by the baby becoming more content and sleeping better), work your way back to the three hour minimum. If no improvement comes, work back to three hours with the aid of a formula compliment for the benefit of your baby and your own peace of mind.

2. If You Question Your Milk Supply in the Fourth Month. The same basic principles apply to this age category. If your baby is between four and six months of age, and you question your milk supply, try adding a couple of feedings to your daytime routine. One of our mothers, (who is also a pediatrician) felt she was loosing her milk supply at four months. She did two things. She added a fifth feeding to her day and she stopped dieting. In less than one week her milk supply was back to normal. Other mothers found success by returning to a fairly tight three hour schedule. Once their milk supply returned to normal they gradually returned to their previous routine. If no improvement comes after five to seven days consider a formula compliment. Adding a few extra feedings during the day is not a setback in your parenting, but it is necessary to insure the healthy balance between breast feeding and the related benefits of PDF.

The Four Day Test. You may also want to consider the four day test. This involves offering a complementary feeding of one to two ounces of formula after each nursing period. Then, express your milk manually or with a breast pump (an electric pump, preferably), ten minutes per side. Keep track of how much extra you are producing. If your milk is plentiful, then the problem lies with your baby. He or she is either not latching on properly or is a lazy nurser. If your milk supply increases as a result of pumping, which will be indicated either by milk expressed or by your baby not wanting the complementary feeding, then return to breast-feeding only, maintaining a three-hour routine.

If the additional stimulation from breast pumping doesn't increase your milk supply, and if you reviewed all the external factors and found them compatible with nursing, then you are probably part of the five percent of moms who can't provide a sufficient milk supply. The solution is not to be found in more nursing, using elaborate lactation aids, sleeping with your baby, or wearing him or her in a sling all day. We recommend you use formula and maintain your routine.

Questions for Review

1. List some variables influencing your routine and desire to beast feed.

2. What is the Healthy Baby Growth Chart? What purpose does it serve?

3. Describe the difference between slow weight gain and "failure to thrive" babies.

4. What is a symptom of an underlying medical problem in a baby? Describe the condition.

5. What should you do if by the end of the third week your baby is not going $2^{1}/2$ to 3 hours on mothers milk?

Chapter Seven

Establishing Your Baby's Routine

hether you have one baby, twins, or a set of triplets, you need to begin establishing your routine from day one. Your baby's routine is a twenty-four-hour strategy designed to meet his or her needs, as well as those of the rest of the family. The strategy we recommend is made up of three basic activities that repeat themselves throughout the day: feeding time, waketime, and naptime. Feeding must be first, waketime second, and naptime third. Do not change that order, with the exception of the late-night and the middle-of-the-night feedings when a waketime is not necessary.

As mentioned in Chapter 3, the first application of your parenting philosophy will show up in the way you choose to feed your baby. During those moments of nurturing, you are doing more than just filling up a little tummy; you are integrating life into your child and your child into life. This process requires a plan. Whether nourishment is passed to your baby by breast or bottle, the guidelines for success are listed below. Add a dose of common sense and you will be well on your way to success.

Your Lifestyle and Your Baby

In Chapter 1, we stated one of our most basic beliefs about child-rearing: Children should be welcome members of the family and not the center of it. With that truth in mind, we'd like to introduce you to two couples—Rod and Colleen, and Dave and Kim.

Rod and Colleen are very disciplined people. As a couple, they are neat, orderly, precise, and systematic in everything they do. There is a place for everything, and everything is in its place. They rise early. By 6:30 A.M., they have jogged two miles, showered, and are prepared to sit down for breakfast. Dinner is usually at the same time each evening, and the activities of the day are fairly predictable. Their lifestyle represents a *tight routine*.

Dave and Kim are comfortable with a little more flex in their lives. They appreciate things that are neat and orderly, precise and systematic, but consider some types of confusion to be an art form. If the day doesn't turn out as planned, no big deal. Sometimes they rise at 6:30 A.M., other days they sleep longer. Mealtimes are determined more by the activities of the day than any preset schedule. Their lifestyle represents a *loose routine*.

Which couple's personal style do you and your spouse most resemble? Is life quite black and white or are you comfortable with variations in routine? If you're more like Rod and Colleen, you will have a tendency to set a tight feeding schedule. If you are more like Dave and Kim, your feeding periods will have more flex to them. For example, some days the baby will receive his first feeding at 6:30 A.M.; other days, it may be at 7:00 A.M. In that case, Kim automatically adjusts the baby's morning routine, based on the timing of the first feeding.

You can take comfort in the knowledge that regardless of your parenting style, in the early weeks and months your baby will adjust to your personality and routine.

Your Baby's First Year

Your baby's first year is divided into four basic phases—phase one: *Stabilization;* phase two: *Extended Night;* phase three: *Extended Day;* and phase four: *Extended Routine.* In this chapter, our focus will be confined to feeding times and associated activities as they relate to each phase. In the next chapter, we will focus on waketime activities and naptime.

Phase One: Stabilization
Birth through Eight Weeks

During the first ten days to two weeks, the daily routine for most new mothers will be a continual repeat of a two-and-a-half- to three-hour cycle, from the end of one feeding to the beginning of the next.

There are a few basic goals to achieve during this phase, for both mom and baby. For the breast-feeding mother, the establishment of stable milk production is the main objective. For the baby, the stabilization of hunger metabolism and sleep/wake cycles are the primary goals. Another goal may be teaching your baby how to nurse. By the end of the eighth week, the baby should be sleeping through the night (for seven to eight hours).

One caution we offer new parents is to be aware that their newborn will tend to fall asleep at the breast before being finished nursing. The mother's job is to keep baby awake until the feeding is over.

Rub baby's toes, change his or her diaper, or talk to the baby. Work at trying to keep your infant awake until after the feeding period is completed. If your child forms the habit of taking in partial feedings, he or she will end up hungry all the time.

General Guidelines

Don't underestimate the following six guidelines. Although simple, they will bring order to your life and will make you a confident and more competent parent.

Understand how to calculate time between feedings.

1. The time between feedings can be measured from the beginning of one feeding to the beginning of the next, or from the end of one feeding to the end of the next. For example, a three-hour feeding cycle means that three hours elapse from the beginning of one feeding period to the beginning of the next. (As previously stated, in practice, a three-hour routine means you will feed your baby two-and-a-half hours after the end of the previous feeding. When you add in the twenty to thirty minutes required for feeding, you complete the three-hour cycle.) For example, two-week-old Ryan received a feeding at 7:00 A.M. His mom nursed him 30 minutes to 7:30 A.M. Ryan is scheduled to receive his next feeding in $2\frac{1}{2}$ hours, which will be at approximately 10:00 A.M. Thus, 3 hours have elapsed from the start of one feeding to the start of the next.

2. Starting with the early morning feeding and continuing through the mid-evening feeding, all three activities will take place: feeding time, waketime, and naptime. But during the late evening and nighttime segment, there should be no extended wake periods.

Feed your baby and put him or her right back to bed.

3. For the first four weeks: Starting with your early morning feeding and continuing through the midevening feeding, generally speaking the time between each nursing period will fall somewhere between $2\frac{1}{2}$ and 3 hours from the end of the last feeding. Any time increment between $2\frac{1}{2}$ and 3 hours is acceptable. During these early weeks, you should stay close to these recommended times. These routine feedings will help to establish and stabilize both lactation and your baby's metabolism. You want to average 8 feedings (7 minimum) in a 24-hour period.

> NOTE: If you need to awaken your baby during the day to prevent him or her from sleeping longer than the three-and-a-half-hour cycle, do so! Such parental intervention is necessary to help stabilize the baby's digestive metabolism. The exception to this guideline comes with the late-evening and nighttime feedings. There is no need to awaken your baby during the night. Let her wake naturally, and then feed her and put her back to bed.

4. Starting with your early morning feeding and continuing through the midevening feeding, the usual time between each nursing period will fall somewhere between two and one-half and three and one-half hours. Any time increment between those two times is acceptable. Given those time increments, plan into your day seven to eight feedings.

5. When you establish your baby's routine, first consider all of your regular activities—such as grocery shopping, work, exercise, household chores, and church attendance. There will be times when

your baby's routine will change to fit into your schedule. At other times you will plan your activity around your baby's needs, simply because it is more practical to do so.

6. Determine the time of the first feeding of the day. That time will be fairly consistent each day and may initially be set by both you and your baby.

Summary of Phase One

By the end of eight weeks, the stabilization phase is complete. By then, your baby should be sleeping through the night on a regular basis. By "sleeping through the night," we are referring to seven to eight hours of uninterrupted sleep. "Regular basis" means continuing in that pattern for at least three consecutive days. That may occur any time between the tenth day and the eighth week, with the average PDF baby sleeping through the night by the sixth week.

NOTE: If your baby is not sleeping through the night by eight weeks, don't worry about it. Although rare, two to three percent of PDF babies begin sleeping through the night at ten and eleven weeks. When they do, they sleep ten hours a night, catching up to all the other PDF babies.

The average number of feedings in a twenty-four-hour period will be seven to eight before your baby is sleeping through the night, and six to eight feedings afterwards. Although you will be dropping the nighttime feeding at this point, you will not be reducing your baby's caloric intake, just rearranging the time of intake. You may need to maintain a seventh or eigthth feeding period for four to five days after your baby initially begins sleeping through. Sticking close to a two-half to three hour routine will help facilitate that goal. Some mothers find those times more in line with their comfort zone and stay there several weeks. Most PDF moms are comfortable alternating between a two and one-half and three and one-half hour routine, getting in six good nursing periods. We'll expand on this point on the next page.

Feeding at Intervals Less Than Two and One-half Hours

As stated, your baby's normal feeding periods fall between two and one-half and three hour intervals. But there are times when you may feed sooner than those time increments. For example, the late afternoon for many nursing mothers is usually when their milk supply is at its lowest point quantitatively and qualitatively. That is usually due to the busyness of the day. As a result, there may be an early evening feeding that occurs as soon as two hours.

Your late evening feeding, the one that falls between 8:30 p.m. and midnight is another example of when you might drop below the two and one-half hour mark. Some mothers feed their babies at 8:30 p.m. and then again at 10:30 p.m. Here the decision to feed within two hours is a practical one—now both Mom and baby can go to bed earlier.

The point is this: it's okay to deviate from the two and one-half to three hour feeding norm. But do not deviate so often that you establish a new norm.

What should you do if your baby sleeps through the night only to awaken at 5:00 A.M., while his normal routine does not start until

6:30 A.M.? You have three choices. The first choice is to wait ten to fifteen minutes to make sure he is truly awake. He may be passing through an active sleep state, moving to deeper sleep. A second possibility is to feed your baby and then put him back down. You can then awaken him at 7:00 A.M. and feed him again. Although that is less than three hours and he may not take much at that feeding, the advantage will be that your baby stays on his morning routine. A third option is to offer a feeding at 5:00 A.M., treating that as your first feeding of the day. In that case, you would adjust the rest of the baby's morning schedule so that by early afternoon he is back on his daily routine.

Considering Context and Being Flexible

Do not be a legalistic parent. Legalists create prohibitions by elevating a method over a principle. They fail to consider the context of a given situation, stubbornly citing rules instead. We have all heard the cliché "Let's keep things in context." The most notable aspect of a legalist is that he or she rejects context. Responding to the context of a situation does not mean suspending the principles of PDF. Rather, you are able to focus on the right response in the short term without compromising your long-term objectives.

As stated above, there will be times when a situation will dictate a temporary suspension of the guidelines presented. Remember, you are the parent, endowed with experience, wisdom, and common sense. Trust these attributes first, not an extreme of emotion or the rigidity of the clock. When special situations arise, allow context to be your guide.

Here are some examples of context and PDF flexibility:

1. Your two-week-old baby boy was sleeping contentedly until his older brother decided to visit him. He is now awake and crying, with another thirty minutes left before his next scheduled feeding. What should you do? You can first try settling the baby back down by patting him on the back or holding him. Placing him in his infant seat is a second option. A third option is to feed him and rework the next feed/wake/nap cycle. (Also, instruct the older brother to check with you before he visits his sleeping sibling.)

2. You are on an airplane and your infant daughter begins to fuss—loudly. You fed her just two hours earlier. What should you do? The answer is simple: consider others. Don't let your baby's routine get in the way of being thoughtful toward others. Failure to act will stress you and the rest of the passengers. You might play with your baby, entertain her, or feed her. Although you normally would not offer food before three hours have passed since the previous feeding, the context of the situation dictates that you suspend your normal routine. When you arrive at your destination, get back to your basic routine. That's the balance!

3. You have been driving for four hours, which is your baby son's normal time between feedings. Your baby is still asleep and you have another forty minutes to travel. As a parent in control, you may choose to awaken your baby and feed him, or wait until you get to your destination.

4. You just fed your baby daughter and dropped her off at the church nursery or with your baby-sitter. You are planning to return within an hour and a half. Should you leave a bottle of breast milk or formula, just in case? The answer is yes. Baby-sitters and nursery

workers provide a valuable service to young parents. Because their care extends to other children, they should not be obligated to follow your routine exactly as you do. If your baby fusses, you will want the caretaker to have the option of offering a bottle (even though it will have been less than three hours). It won't throw your child off her routine to receive early feedings a few times during the week.

Most of your day will be fairly routine and predictable. But there will be times when you may need more flexibility, due to unusual circumstances. Your life will be less tense if you consider the context of each situation and respond appropriately for the benefit of everyone. Right parental responses often determine whether their child is a blessing to others, or a source of discomfort.

Sample Schedule

Below, we have provided a sample schedule that you can personalize for yourself and your baby. Remember the basic rule: Feed every two-and-a-half to three hours after the end of the last feeding, then have a waketime, followed by a naptime. The various activities listed alongside the waketimes are suggestions. This work sheet is based on seven to eight feedings in a twenty-four-hour period, and is a guide for your first six to eight weeks.

FEEDING	WHAT TO DO
Early Morning	
_____a.m.	1. Feeding and diaper change.
	2. Waketime: Rock your baby and sing; place your baby on his or her back in the crib to watch a mobile.

3. Put your baby down for a nap.

Mid-morning
_____a.m.

1. Feeding and diaper change.
2. Waketime: Take a walk with your baby, run errands, or visit neighbors.
3. Put your baby down for a nap.

Afternoon
_____p.m.

1. Feeding and diaper change.
2. Waketime: Bathe your baby and place him or her in an infant seat near a window.
3. Put your baby down for a nap.

Mid-afternoon
_____p.m.

1. Feeding and diaper change.
2. Waketime: Play with your baby; have him or her by your side as you read or sew.
3. Put your baby down for a nap.

Late Afternoon
_____p.m.

1. Feeding and diaper change.
2. Wake time: Family time.
3. Put your baby down for a nap.

Early Evening
_____p.m.

• Feeding, diaper change, (possible wake time) then put your baby back to bed.

Late Evening

_____p.m.
- Feeding and diaper change, then put your baby back to bed. (NOTE: This will be your last scheduled feeding of the day. Don't wake your baby from this point on. Let him or her wake up naturally.)

Nighttime

_____a.m.
- Feeding and diaper change, then put your baby back to bed.

When a breast-fed baby initially begins sleeping through the night, Mom may experience some slight discomfort for the first couple of mornings. For some of these moms, it may take a couple of days for their bodies to make the proper adjustments to the longer nighttime sleep. If this happens to you, compensate for the longer stretch at night by adding an extra feeding or two during the day. As a result of a couple of extra nursing periods, feeding times might drop below the two and one-half hour mark. This will be temporary. Within a week's time both Mom and baby should have adjusted to their new sleep/wake patterns, and extra feedings are ususally not necessary.

Phase Two: Extended Night
Weeks Nine through Fifteen

During this second phase, a breast-fed baby can extend his nighttime sleep nine to ten hours, while a bottle-fed baby can go eleven hours. Make a note of this fact: Breast-feeding mothers must stay mindful of their milk production. Letting your baby sleep longer than nine or ten hours at night may not afford you enough time during the day for sufficient stimulation. That is not true for all mothers but is for some. Therefore, if you're breast feeding and are concerned about a decrease in your milk supply we recommend that you not let your baby sleep longer than ten hours at night during this phase.

Bedtime during this phase will be adjusted closer to the early-evening feeding. By the end of the thirteenth week, your baby should average five to six feedings a day, but never less than four.

Phase Three: Extended Day
Weeks Sixteen through Twenty-four

Usually between the sixteenth and twenty-fourth weeks, you will introduce your baby to solid foods. Your pediatrician will direct you in that area. During phase three, most babies are sleeping ten to eleven hours at night. Again, breast-feeding mothers must continually monitor their milk supply. If you feel you need to add an additional feeding during the day, do it.

By the twenty-fourth week your baby's mealtimes should begin to line up with the rest of the family's: breakfast, lunch, and dinner, with a fourth, fifth, and for some, a sixth liquid feeding at bedtime. As you begin introducing solids to your baby's diet, please note that you are not adding more feeding periods, just additional food at breakfast, lunch, and dinner. For example, at breakfast you will give cereal, then breast-or bottle-feed. Do not offer cereal alone with a supplemental liquid feeding two hours later. That would mean you are feeding every two hours, which is not a helathy habit. Introducing solid foods is a topic discussed in detail in *Babywise II, Parenting Your Pre-toddler.*

As a breast-feeding mother, try to maintain four to six feeding periods as long as you are nursing; any less may decrease your milk supply.

Phase Four: Extended Routine
Weeks Twenty-five through Fifty-two

Between the ages of six months and twelve months, your baby will continue to feed on three meals a day. Each meal is supplemented by baby food, with an optional fourth liquid feeding before bed. At this age, your baby should be taking two naps averaging from one-and-a-half to two-and-a-half hours in length. Continue with four to five nursing periods during the day. This same general rule applies to formula-fed babies (see Chapter 5, "Facts on Feeding").

Summary of First-Year Feeding

For easy reference, the following summary of your baby's first year of feeding is provided.

Phase One: Weeks One through Eight

Start with seven to eight daily feedings for the first two months. The number of feedings will depend on whether you begin with a strict three-hour routine or a more flexible three- to three-and-a-half-hour routine. By the end of this phase, you should be averaging six to seven feedings in a twenty-four-hour period, and most likely will not have a middle-of-the-night feeding.

Phase Two: Weeks Nine through Fifteen

You will transition from six to seven feedings down to five to six feedings in a twenty-four-hour period. By week thirteen, most babies easily go to a combination of three and one-half- to four hour routine, and drop the late-evening feeding.

Phase Three: Weeks Sixteen through Twenty-four

Your baby will maintain four to six liquid feedings in a twenty-four hour period, three of which will be supplemented with baby food.

Phase Four: Weeks Twenty-five through Fifty-two

The process of moving a child to three meals a day should be nearly completed by the beginning of this phase. Remember that at each meal there needs to be a time of nursing, plus a fourth nursing period just before bed.

How to Drop a Feeding

By dropping a feeding, we don't mean your baby will take in less food over a twenty-four-hour period. Actually, the amount will gradually increase, although the frequency of feedings will decrease. As your baby begins to take more food at each feeding and his metabolism stabilizes, you will begin dropping a feeding period. The three most common ways to do this are by:

1. *Changing from a three-hour to a three-and-a-half-hour schedule, or from a three-and-a-half-hour to a four-hour schedule.* If you have to consistently wake your baby for his or her daytime feedings, this is a

strong indication the baby can go longer between feedings. Generally, your baby will be capable of moving to a flexible three to four hour routine by three months of age.

2. *Dropping the middle-of-the-night feeding.* Many babies drop this feeding on their own between the sixth and eighth week. One night they simply sleep until morning. Some babies gradually stretch the distance between the 10:00 P.M. and the 6:00 A.M. feedings. If you hear your baby stirring or beginning to cry, wait a little while (five to fifteen minutes) before attending to him or her. At this age, the baby is waking more out of conditioning (his or her biological clock) than from a need for food or comfort.

There are some little ones whose internal clocks get "stuck" at the nighttime feeding. Parental guidance can help reset that clock. If you have a digital timepiece and notice that your baby is waking at nearly the same time each night, that's a strong indicator that his or her biological clock is stuck. To correct the problem, wait for a weekend when no one has to get up early for work. (You may want to sleep in if your sleep is disturbed by your baby's crying during the night.) When your baby awakens, don't rush right in to him or her. Any crying will be temporary, lasting from five to forty-five minutes. Remember, *this will be temporary!* Some parents fear that failing to respond right away will make their baby feel unloved or insecure. On the contrary, it's cruel not to help your child gain the skill of sleeping through the night. Taking the baby into bed with you will delay the learning process.

Generally, it takes three nights to establish a new routine, one that allows for continuous sleep for both mom and baby.

3. *Dropping the late-evening feeding.* This process occurs anywhere from two months of age on, and is usually the trickiest feeding to

eliminate. Having grown accustomed to sleeping all night, some parents are reluctant to drop the late-evening feeding for fear that the baby will awaken in the middle of the night, starving.

Sometimes, in the process of eliminating feedings, bending a guideline may be necessary. If we assume your baby is on a four-hour schedule (6:00 A.M., 10:00 A.M., 2:00 P.M., 6:00 P.M., and 10:00 P.M.), and you think he or she is ready to drop the last feeding, then instead of eliminating the 10:00 P.M. feeding completely, try backing it up fifteen minutes per day until you arrive at the time you desire. For a while, your baby's last two feedings of the day may be less than three hours apart, which is permissible during this transition time.

The rest of the day's schedule may need to be adjusted so that you end up with a new four-hour format which looks like this: feedings at 8:00 A.M., 12:00 P.M., 4:00 P.M., and 8:00 P.M. (or whatever times best suit your family).

Questions for Review

1. List the three activities of your baby's routine.

   a.

   b.

   c.

2. From the list above, what exception applies to the late-evening and middle-of-the-night feedings?

3. What are the two ways you can measure the time between feedings?

4. When should you wake a sleeping baby, and when should you let him sleep?

5. Responding to context helps you do what?

Chapter Eight

Waketime And Naptime

*I*n this chapter we will examine the last two activities in your baby's routine: waketime and naptime. One common mistake made when following a routine is to reverse the order of these last two activities—that is, putting the baby down for a nap right after his or her feeding. Because newborns tend to be sleepy, you will initially have to work at keeping your baby awake during feedings and for a short period thereafter. If you switch naptime and waketime, you will be wondering why your baby cries so much.

We discourage parents from allowing their babies to fall asleep without having received a full feeding. You can keep that from happening by including a diaper change halfway through the feeding, by making sure your baby is not too warm (warmth induces sleep), or by placing a cool, damp face cloth on your baby's feet. Don't bounce or jiggle your infant in an attempt to keep him or her awake.

If nothing works, put your baby down to sleep, but don't feed him or her before the start of the next cycle. This is one of the only times when the clock can authoritatively guide a feeding decision. Teach your baby how and when to eat. Babies learn very quickly how to become snackers, but they will just as easily learn how to take a complete meal. Either way, the parent guides the results.

etime

Waketime activities include times when you and your baby will be together and times when your baby will explore his or her new world alone. One thing is certain: Your baby does not need to be entertained by you all day long.

Mom, Dad, and Baby Together

Feeding: Whether bottle- or breast-feeding, you will spend much of your day holding your baby while feeding him or her.

Singing: At birth, a baby responds to his or her mom and dad's voices. Talk and sing to your baby during waketimes, remembering that learning is always taking place.

Reading: It's never too soon to read to your baby or to show the baby colorful picture books (especially cardboard or plastic ones that the baby can explore more on his or her own). Your infant loves to hear the sound of your voice and inflections.

Bathing: This is another pleasant routine for you and your baby. You can sing, tell your child which part of his or her body you are washing, or just have fun splashing.

Walking: Taking time for a stroll outside is great for you and your little one. You can sing or talk while you are walking, and the fresh air is good for both of you.

Playing: Initially, you can't play much with a newborn. A few early play activities are: flirting with your baby, smiling, talking, and gently moving his or her arms and legs and of course cuddling with your newborn. That is more than fun; it is a necessary way to express physical love to him or her.

Baby Alone

Pictures: Putting bright pictures and patterns around the nursery is a great way to stimulate your baby visually.

Mobiles: Moving, musical mobiles help your baby learn to track with his or her eyes.

Gym: Crib gyms and objects that dangle over your baby and rattle when he or she bats at them, help to develop her hand-eye coordination. Batting is the necessary preparation for reaching out and holding objects. (For safety's sake, the crib gym should not be dangled over the baby once the child learns to sit up.)

Swing: Putting a baby in a swing allows your infant to watch what is going on around him or her. Swings are especially helpful for calming fussy newborns. However, don't get into the habit of letting your baby fall asleep in a swing, since the child needs to learn to fall asleep without this prop.

Infant Seat: This item provides another way you can help your baby to sit up and take notice of the world. Sometimes toys or books can be hung from an overhead handle.

Playpen: Start at one month of age with the playpen. A four-week-old baby can spend some waketime in an infant seat placed inside the playpen in view of a mobile. Also, allow the child to take a nap in the playpen once in a while.

Having some of this equipment—whether new, used, or borrowed—is helpful, but it is certainly not a necessity. In addition to feeding, changing, and bathing your baby, you might have at least one playtime a day when the baby has your full attention for fifteen minutes or so. Dad also needs to spend time each day with the baby, in addition to possible feeding times.

Naptime

Naps are not an option based on your baby's wants. When naptime comes, the baby goes down. It is that simple. For optimal development, infants need daytime rest. While following your feeding, wake, and sleep routine, you should plan that the last 1½ to 2 hours of your 3-hour cycle will be for a nap. When moving to a 3½ to 4-hour routine, your baby's naps will range anywhere from 1½ to 2½ hours.

NOTE: If your baby during the first two months is not napping well, try cutting back on his waketime by 15-minute increments. Some babies become over-stimulated during waketime and have difficulty settling in for a nap. The fatigued or over-stimulated child becomes hyper-alert fighting off sleep through crying. If this is a regular problem for your baby, shorten his waketime.

There may be a brief period of fussing or crying when you put the baby down for a nap. Don't be deterred from doing what is best for the child. Crying isn't the terrible beast that some of the last generation of medical practitioners thought it was. Some crying is a normal part of a baby's day and some babies will cry a few minutes in the process of settling themselves to sleep. The future trade-off will be a baby who goes down for a nap without fussing and wakes up cooing.

Crying for 15-20 or even 30 minutes is not going to hurt your baby physically or emotionally. Your baby will not lose brain cells, experience a drop in IQ, or have feelings of rejection that will leave him manic-depressive at age thirty. You do not undo all the love and care of the waking hours with a few minutes of crying. On the other hand, if you want a fussy baby, never let him cry, and hold, rock, and feed him as soon as he starts to fuss. We guarantee you will achieve your goal.

Sleeping Patterns

Unlike feeding patterns, infant sleep behavior has more variation due to individual differences. Remember, stable sleep patterns are based on stable hunger patterns. When there are a number of changes in your baby's eating patterns, there will be corresponding changes in his sleep patterns.

Newborn

Newborns will sleep sixteen to twenty hours per day, including the periods of sleep between each feeding. Under parent directed feeding, this sleep will come in six to eight naps (depending on the number of daily feedings). For the first couple of weeks, your baby may be very sleepy. You will need to work at keeping him awake during feeding times. When your baby has been up for the appropriate duration and begins to show signs of fussiness, it is time for a nap.

Avoid letting your baby just snack at mealtimes. Frequent snacking during the day is the enemy of nighttime sleep. If your baby falls asleep at the breast, even after your best efforts to keep him awake, then put him down for a nap. He may sleep until the next feeding, but do not let him sleep longer. Wake him for his feeding. On the other hand, if your baby starts waking too soon between feedings, then you will need to work harder to keep him awake longer before putting him down for a nap.

Two Months

If you follow the principles of PDF, this will be the period when your baby drops his or her nighttime feeding and begins sleeping seven to eight hours continuously. Naps during the day should be at least one-and-a-half hours long. Seventy percent of PDF babies drop the middle-of-the-night feeding on their own. The remaining thirty percent need a little nudge. This may involve some crying, which might continue for as little as five minutes or last as long as one hour, off and on. It usually takes three days to establish unbroken sleep cycles at this age.

> NOTE: It's not unusual for two- or three-month-old PDF babies to awaken at around 5:00 or 5:30 a.m. and talk to themselves for up to an hour. Afterward, they usually go back to sleep for another hour or so. This quirky phase can go on for a week or up to a month. If you start to respond each time you hear a noise from the cradle, then 5:00 a.m. will become your baby's waketime—and yours, too.

Three to Five Months

During this period, your baby will drop his or her late-evening feeding, leaving four to six feeding periods during the day. Nighttime sleep will average ten to twelve hours. The baby will have three day-time naps between one-and-a-half to two hours in length, resulting in a longer waketime. Once the third nap is dropped, both waketime and the remaining naptimes will increase in duration.

Six to Sixteen Months

Your baby will drop his late-afternoon/early-evening nap at around six months of age, leaving two naptimes—one in the morning and one in the afternoon. The naps are usually each about two hours long. (For more information on this period of development, please read *BABYWISE II*.)

Sixteen Months and Older

Between sixteen and twenty months, the morning nap is dropped. Your baby should be sleeping ten to twelve hours at night and two to three hours during one afternoon nap.

Waking Up Happy

Between four and six months of age, infants generally develop a wakeup disposition—one that you highly influence. Your baby's disposition can be happy and content when you follow three basic rules for naps.

Rule 1: Mom, not the baby, decides when the nap starts.

Rule 2: Mom, not the baby, decides when the nap ends.

Rule 3: If your baby wakes up crying or cranky, it's most often because he or she has not had sufficient sleep. Other factors to consider are a dirty diaper, a noisy neighbor, sickness coming on, or an arm or leg stuck between the crib slats.

After having been put down for a nap, your baby will move from an active sleep state to relaxed sleep in thirty to forty-five minutes. In the next thirty to forty-five minutes, he or she will move from relaxed sleep back to active sleep. At the end of that cycle, your baby may begin to stir and cry. Parents often interpret this to mean naptime is over. Going in to pick up the baby, they assume the child's crankiness is his or her natural way of waking up. But that's not the case.

If your baby is waking up cranky or crying, he or she most likely is not getting enough sleep. Even though he or she may cry, your baby will probably go right back to sleep in ten minutes for another thirty to forty minutes of rest. When your baby gets enough sleep, you will notice a happy disposition; the baby will make happy cooing sounds, letting you know it's time to get him or her up.

Summary

When your baby starts to sleep through the night, people will invariably say, "You're just lucky," or "You've got an easy baby." Neither statement is true. Your baby is sleeping through the night because you trained him or her to do so. You can take the credit for your success. But do keep this fact in perspective: Getting your baby to sleep through the night is not the final goal of parenting—but we believe it does represent a right beginning.

Questions for Review

1. What common mistake is made in relation to waketime and naptime?

2. In the first month, your baby may be very sleepy. What are some things you can do to keep him or her awake?

3. In relation to the previous question, if your baby doesn't stay awake, what should you do?

4. Are naps optional for infants? Please explain.

5. When you follow a feeding, waketime, and sleeping routine, how much time should be devoted for a nap in a three-hour cycle? In a four-hour cycle?

6. Summarize the three "Wake Up Happy" rules.

   a.

   b.

   c.

7. What is the most common reason for your baby to wake up cranky or crying?

Chapter Nine

When Your Baby Cries

hy do babies cry? Shakespeare's King Lear said, "When we are born we cry that we are come to this great stage of fools." While this is clever and poetic, in reality, a baby's crying is much more complex than that! When a baby cries and gnaws at his or her hands, we often assume he must be hungry and should be fed. There are many reasons babies cry, but hunger often is the only reason people consider. Besides crying when they are hungry, babies cry when they are tired, wet, sick, bored, frustrated, out of their routine, fed too often, or sometimes, simply because that is what normal, healthy babies do. As a parent, you must learn to assess your baby's cry so you can respond properly.

The Power of a Cry

An infant's cry has a great influence on his or her development, not because of the cry itself but because of how the parents respond. Throughout the day, your baby has definite needs for you to meet. You shouldn't define his or her needs so much by the fact your baby is crying as by your *assessment* of what that cry means. Assessment is important.

In early infancy, crying is an intuitive way of communicating both need and displeasure. Cries vary in purpose and intensity. The hunger cry is different from the sick cry. The sleepy cry is different from the "cuddle me" cry. And the distress cry differs from the demanding cry. Crying varies in volume, too. Sometimes a cry will be nothing more than a gentle whimper; other times, it's a violent protest. Attempts to minimize or block all crying can easily increase stress rather than decrease it, especially in light of the fact that emotional tears carry away from the body chemically-activated stress hormones.

Those who are most affected by a baby's cry are the parents (although parents possess a greater cry tolerance than grandparents do). No parent takes pleasure in hearing that sound, and neither will you. This is especially true if you are a first-time parent, because you have never experienced as powerful an emotion as the one caused by your baby's cry. It's a sound that can cause you to wonder if you have done something wrong. You will feel that way, not because crying itself is bad, but because you will be unfamiliar with the emotions of uncertainty that crying evokes.

Teaching Your Baby to Love, or...?

Does responding immediately with breast-feeding to a baby's every cry–on–cue teach him or her how to love? Does *not* responding to every cry with breast-feeding teach disappointment? We believe this kind of thinking reduces love and security to a process, rather than a relationship.

There is no evidence to prove that an immediate response to

every cry teaches a baby anything about love, just as there is no evidence to prove that a little crying fosters feelings of insecurity. A child learns love and gains security from the total context of the parent-child relationship, not from any one action.

Experience teaches us that parents who desire to demonstrate true love to their children will put aside their own emotions for the sake of the child. They will tolerate a little crying if, by their assessment, doing so is the best plan of action for the baby—such as when a baby needs to settle in for a nap or a restful night's sleep.

The Inevitable Conflict

Does crying create within a baby irreversible latent effects on personality development that will surface years later, as suggested by attachment theorists? Should we equate human offspring with animal offspring, as Darwin suggests? We believe the answer is no, on both counts. The question isn't whether crying is bad for your baby, but whether blocking *all* crying is good for him. The answer to this question, too, is no! By persisting with a "block that cry" mind-set, a mother loses confidence in her own ability to make decisions about the child later. Furthermore, there isn't a great amount of difference between blocking a baby's cry by offering food at each whimper, and wearing him or her in a sling all day so the baby won't cry.

A mom who picks up her baby and offers the breast each time he or she cries is teaching her baby that food is the source of comfort, not mom. This explains why Marisa—the fed-on-demand baby we introduced in Chapter 1—is not easily comforted by secondary caregivers. It may also may help explain the obesity problem with our nation's youth, and why so many adults turn to food for stress relief; they have been trained that way from the beginning. We are not trying to express an inevitable cause-and-effect relationship between a fat baby and a fat adolescent later on. But poor eating habits in infancy, such as overfeeding or disregarding healthy eating patterns, may result in eventual obesity.

There is another consideration. What will happen to Marisa, whose parents have conditioned her to expect immediate gratification, when it is no longer possible to satisfy her immediately? What happens when the second or third child comes into the family? Think of the emotional trauma she will experience then. This painful experience is described by mothers as the child becoming "completely unglued." The child has been so conditioned to immediate response that he or she simply can't cope with a delayed response. Now the child is emotionally fragile, rather than emotionally stable.

Marisa's mom has been bombarded by clichés such as, "You can't hurt a baby by picking her up whenever she cries," or "You can't spoil her by loving her too much." Of course you can hurt a baby by picking him or her up too much. Chelsea's mother (Chelsea is a PDF baby) is more discerning. She realizes that jumping to satisfy her daughter's every cry would result in a child with a *predisposition for requiring immediate gratification,* which would become a destructive influence on her daughter's pretoddler and toddler development. Immediate-gratification training negatively impacts a child's ability to learn the skills of sitting, focusing, and concentrating. Right-learning experiences lead to right-learning patterns.

Babies not only become conditioned to being picked up at a whimper, but they also become abnormally dependent on it. How sad to think that Marisa's parents are unknowingly training her to use crying as her only mode of expression.

The PDF Baby

It is commonly observed that babies under the parent-directed-feeding plan tend to cry less in the long run than babies who are demand-fed. The reason? Infants put on a routine become confident and secure in that routine. Their lives have order, and they learn the lesson of flexibility early in life.

Babies who settle into regular and predictable rhythms of activity develop greater tolerance to frustration and learn to use modes of communication other than crying. Chelsea expresses herself with happy sounds, such as cooing, and by excited body motions, such as bouncing. These are additional modes of "baby talk."

Cries to Listen For

Some crying is normal and should be expected, but there are certain identifiable cries which you will want to be alert for.[1] A high-pitched, piercing cry may be a signal of either internal or external bodily injury. Such a cry, if persistent, should be brought to the attention of your pediatrician.

A marked change in your baby's crying pattern—such as a sudden increase in the frequency and duration of crying, or a weak, mousy cry—may be a warning of illness. Be sure to discuss this with your pediatrician. Cries indicating hunger or thirst are predictable with PDF babies. You can be sure what you hear is not a hunger-and-thirst cry if your baby is satisfied after a feeding. With demand-fed babies, cries are unpredictable, leaving mom and dad guessing and anxious.

Babies who cry routinely and act hungry after two hours are probably not getting enough food. If you are breast-feeding, check your milk supply and the factors which influence it. (See the section subtitled "Testing Your Milk Supply" in Chapter 6.)

Answering Your Baby's Cry

"How long should I let my baby cry?" is the most common question asked by new moms. Answering that question isn't difficult, once you know how to identify both legitimate and illegitimate cry periods. The timing of your baby's cry is the first clue to understanding how you should respond. During the first four months of life, there are six possible cry periods, three of which are classified abnormal and three normal.

Abnormal cry times include crying:

a) during feedings;
b) immediately after feedings;
c) at times when baby wakes early out of a sound nap.

Crying during any one of these periods requires attention. Don't wait for the crying to subside; investigate, looking for the root cause. These are not trainable cry periods, such as those times when you put your baby down for a nap; they come about due to legitimate need.

Crying During Feeding. Crying during feeding might occur if your baby isn't getting enough food or isn't taking in food fast enough. There could be a number of reasons for these conditions, including improper latching-on or a poor milk release. (Please see Chapter 6, "Monitoring Your Baby's Growth.")

Crying Immediately after Feeding. If your baby cries routinely within thirty minutes after his or her feeding, and the cry sounds like a pain cry rather than a sleepiness cry, it may be caused by one of several factors:

1. *Trapped gas.* Young babies often swallow air during feedings, air which must be brought up again. Burp your baby by holding him or her against your shoulder, on your lap, or over your knee.

2. *Your diet.* Consider what you are eating if you are breast-feeding. Be careful to avoid eating too many dairy products or spicy foods. You don't have to completely eliminate these foods from your diet, but you may have to cut back considerably.

3. *A milk quality problem.* A breast-feeding mother can have a sufficient quantity of milk but at the same time not have a sufficient *quality* of milk. As a result, the baby responds with a hunger cry cue within an hour. Although this condition is relatively rare, it may affect as many as five percent of nursing mothers.

Waking Early Out of a Sound Nap. If your baby wakes out of a sound sleep with a strong cry, it may be the result of a combination of any of the three factors mentioned above. It might also mean you have too much flexibility in your routine.

Normal Crying Periods

Different from the abnormal cry periods just discussed (which always require your prompt attention), some crying is normal and should be expected. The normal cry periods usually come:

a) just before feeding;
b) when baby is put down for a nap;
c) during the late afternoon/early evening period.

Crying Just before Feeding. Under normal circumstances, any crying that occurs just before a feeding should be limited, since the next event for the baby is mealtime. If your baby is hungry, feed him or her. If the child routinely shows signs of hunger before the next scheduled feeding, then find out why, rather than letting the baby cry it out. Your baby's routine is to serve you, you aren't to serve your baby's routine.

Crying When Going Down for a Nap. When putting your baby down for a nap, the duration of crying is set by the child but monitored by the parent. Identifying and knowing your baby's cry patterns and disposition (personal style) will help you learn to discern real needs. Our first grandchild, Ashley, had a cry pattern at naptime that could easily be represented by a gradual bell curve. A gentle whimper built to a mild wail, which then would fall back again to a whimper, followed by sleep. The total time elapsed was ten minutes, with the exception of her late-afternoon cry, which lasted fifteen minutes. By four weeks of age, it took her just five minutes of crying to settle into her nap. Often she would be put down and would fall right off to sleep. Knowing Ashley's cry patterns allowed her mother to be discerning when, one day, at six weeks of age, Ashley cried longer than usual. Recognizing the difference in the length of the cry, Ashley's mother went in, picked her up, and held her for a few moments; then she put her back down. Ashley went off to a contented sleep.

Whitney is Ashley's sister. Her cry patterns were much different. She would wail ten minutes, then stop. About a minute later, she would wail ten minutes more, then stop. A moment after that she would whimper, then sleep. That naptime pattern lasted twelve weeks. Crying for Whitney became an art form, despite the fact that Whitney was nurtured, loved, and cared for with the same intensity as her sister. Whitney didn't have any more or less nutritional or love needs in her life, but she did have by nature a greater disposition for crying. Know your child's cry disposition, and realize that some children have a greater propensity to cry, which is not necessarily a signal that their basic needs are not being met.

Our third grandchild, Katelynn, had yet a different history of crying. She would climb rapidly from a whimper to a wail, like an F-16 heading into the stratosphere, then at the height of her cry, she would stop abruptly and drop off to a sound sleep. Her cry times averaged ten minutes in length at naptime for the first month. After four weeks, she, like her cousin Whitney, became selective as to which naptimes she would cry. After three months, crying at naptime was rare for all three grandchildren; instead, healthy, continuous naptime and nighttime sleep was the norm. Without knowing your child's cry patterns, you will always be second-guessing his or her real need, and you will not know how long your baby's cry period should last.

"But I can't stand to hear my baby cry" is a commonly repeated phrase. If you do not have a goal in mind, i.e. teaching healthy sleep habits, then letting your baby cry before he falls asleep at naptimes makes little sense. The absence of an attainable and measurable goal breeds doubt and confusion. If you have no goal then why are you doing what you are doing? But when you have for a goal the teaching of good sleep habits, some temporary crying is preferable over long-term poor sleep habits.

Some children cry fifteen minutes before falling asleep, others vary their cry amounts from five minutes at one naptime to an off-and-on, thirty-five minute cry at another. If your baby cries longer than fifteen minutes, check on the baby; pat him or her on the back, possibly holding the child for a moment; then put the baby back down. Remember, you aren't training your child not to cry, but are training him or her in the skill of sleep. This is the only time in your baby's day that the practice of nonintervention is best.

Realized early-on are the benefits of healthy sleep training, and those benefits not only come early, but come in multiple forms. A well-rested baby is a good feeder. You will be able to put your baby down for his nap or bedtime and walk away with the child falling asleep and waking with contentment. Another advantage to successful sleep training is that you will be able to put your baby down at anyone's house and have the same success.

Crying During the Late Afternoon/Early Evening Period. Most babies have a personal fussy time. A fussy time in the late afternoon is not uncommon. That's true of both bottle- and breast-fed infants. There is no reason for you to be anxious about your fussy baby, because you are in good company. Literally millions of mothers and fathers are going through the same thing at just about the same time each day.

If a child is not comforted by the baby swing, an infant seat, siblings, or grandma, consider the crib. At least there he has the chance of falling asleep.

If you have a baby who becomes exceptionally and continuously fussy, consider the possibility that he is hungry. How is your milk supply? Are you eating right? Go back to Chapter 5 and look at the factors influencing your milk production. Also, check what you're eating. Hot, spicy foods or a large intake of dairy products can be common contributors to a baby's fussy behavior at any time of the day. Adding the wrong foods to your diet can amplify your baby's normal fussy time and create nightmares for young parents.

Do you remember our two cousins, Chelsea and Marisa? Because Marisa is not on a routine, she is much more likely to be a fussy baby. Chelsea, on the other hand, may have a fussy time, but she will not be characterized as a twenty-four-hour fussy baby.

Don't misinterpret your baby's fussy time as colic. Colic, which basically is a spasm in the baby's intestinal tract that causes pain, is very rare in PDF babies but is intensified in demand-fed babies. The last thing you want to put into an irritated stomach is food, but that is usually the first thing many mothers do. The baby cries, and the mother offers the breast. The baby nurses out of reflex, not because he or she finds comfort in more food.

Very few infants truly suffer from colic. It appears as early as the second week and usually disappears by the end of the twelfth week. Spells of colic usually occur in the early evening, at night, and right after feeding. The baby may draw up his or her legs and clench fists tightly as if in pain. He or she may act hungry but begin crying part way through the feeding.

Contact your pediatrician if these symptoms occur. Having a child that cries for hours for no apparent reason can be very frustrating and emotionally draining on you as a parent. If your baby does suffer from colic, the best thing you can do is to keep the child on a routine that will allow his or her stomach to rest between feedings.

We can't give you a precise time limitation for normal periods of crying. But think carefully about each cry situation, then decide when to intervene and when not to. In time, and as a result of your training, your baby will go down for naps and nighttime sleep contentedly and without crying.

What Should I Do When My Baby Cries?

In relation to a baby's cry, the distinction between feeding philosophies is basic. Chelsea's mom understands the wisdom of first assessing her baby's cry and then acting. She listens, she thinks, and then she acts on her assessment.

Marisa's mom, unfortunately, doesn't take time to assess. In fact, she has been told *not* to think but simply react to her feelings when she hears her baby cry. But feelings are not the basis for sound decision-making. To deny the importance of careful assessment is to deny parents their leadership role. Leaders must be clear-headed and ready to make decisions. They should not be driven by their emotions. In practice, emotional mothering can set the stage for child abuse. How? It creates a vicious cycle. A common characteristic found among abusive parents is a tendency to direct thoughtless, impassioned responses toward their innocent children. Too often those responses are fueled by sleepless nights and a child trained to be demanding.

How should you respond when your baby cries? Unless you sense your baby is in danger, take a moment to listen and assess his or her crying. After a brief assessment, take the appropriate action. Here are some practical, somewhat more detailed, steps to follow.

Listen **for the type of cry.** Even in the early days and weeks, you will begin to distinguish different tones and patterns in your baby's crying. By simply stopping to listen, you may find that the crying ends as quickly as it began. Why listen? If a child has a dirty diaper, are you going to feed him or her? If your baby has trapped gas, is food the answer? If your baby cries because of an ear infection, is nursing what the baby needs?

Think **about where your baby is in his or her routine.** Is naptime finished, or is your baby in the middle of his or her nap and in need of resettling? Does your baby need to go down for a nap? Has she been in the swing too long? Did he lose his toy? Did she spit up? Is this your baby's fussy time of day? This is only a short list of why your baby might be crying. There are many reasons for infant tears other than hunger.

Take action **based on what you have heard and reasonably concluded.** Just remember, sometimes the best "action" to take is no action at all. For example, if your baby is clean, fed, and ready for naptime, let him or her learn how to fall asleep alone, if that's what your baby needs. If you try to nurse your child to sleep, you have only succeeded in manipulating his or her sleep.

Take note of how long your baby cries. It can be comforting later to realize all that noise (which seemed interminable at the time) really lasted only five, ten, or fifteen minutes. If you have listened, waited, and determined that the crying is not subsiding, gather more information by checking on the baby. Peek into his or her crib and see if your baby has become jammed into a corner, in which case you would simply move the baby and offer a gentle pat on the back before leaving the room.

There will be times when your assessment calls for picking up and holding your baby to reassure the child that everything is all right. Some special time in mommy's arms may be all that is needed. Your assessment may produce many options, but blocking your child's cry because you can't handle it shouldn't be one of them.

When Should I Hold and Comfort My Baby?

You will, of course, hold your baby many hours a day as you go through the normal process of caring for and feeding him or her. Flirt with, rock, and sing to your infant when he or she is happy and not so happy, but don't feel you must constantly hold your baby during every fussy time.

Parents should offer comfort to their baby when comfort is needed. The standard question every parent should ask is: What type of comfort should I give my baby right now? A diaper change will comfort a wet baby, a feeding will comfort a hungry baby, holding will comfort a startled baby, and sleep will comfort a tired baby. A baby can receive comfort in many ways and from different people. Certainly dad, older siblings, grandma, and grandpa can be sources of comfort. A baby can be comforted by being held, rocked, sung to, taken for a stroller ride, or placed near a source of music. The good news is that a mother's breasts are not the only source of comfort for a baby.

Wisdom dictates that a mother should recognize that a baby

responds to different forms of comfort at different times. If you use one source exclusively—nursing, for example—you are just stopping the cry and not necessarily comforting your baby.

Summary

As a parent, you will learn to recognize your baby's different cries and will know how to respond with confidence. The wise parent will listen, think, and then take action. If your baby is fed, clean, dry, and healthy, but begins to cry before falling asleep, consider it just one more phase of your child's normal development.

Questions for Review

1. Throughout the day your baby will have definite needs for you to meet. What are the right and wrong ways to define those needs?

2. What are parents teaching an infant when they pick him or her up and offer food each time the baby cries? What problems can result from this practice?

3. List the three abnormal and normal cry periods. What is the general difference between the two?

4. What is wrong with the advice, "When your baby cries, don't think, just react"?

5. What three things should you do when your baby cries?

a.

b.

c.

6. As it relates to comforting a baby, what is the standard question every parent should ask? Give examples.

Chapter Ten

Multiple Birth: The Endless Party

a baby is a great blessing, and multiple births represent multiplied blessings to parents. But with twins, triplets, or quadruplets, your joy will be accompanied by a great deal of work. This is a matter of simple addition. (No, make that multiplication!)

All parenting requires organization and thinking ahead. However, when you bring home a multiple birth, you *really* have to think and plan, because when the unexpected happens, *it happens in multiples*. People with a single baby make their mistakes one at a time; parents of triplets often make their mistakes in triplicate. On the bright side, when you do things right, you have success in multiples, too.

At our house we like to think of parenting our triplets as the party that never ends. When our three boys were tiny preemies and needed feeding every three hours, we saw feeding times as an opportunity for family fun and fellowship. The feeders would sit together in the same room and discuss their day, tell jokes or stories, or sing songs. Even at 3 A.M., we feeders were encouraged in our toil by our mutual commitment to see this as an opportunity to socialize.

From the earliest age, children will sense your attitude. If you approach their care as if it is a burden of drudgery, then your children will respond in a burdensome way and you will experience drudgery. Instead, see each day as an adventure and know that each stage of your children's development is precious.

Bringing Them Home

Multiple-birth pregnancies are at high risk for prematurity. Therefore, a major challenge early on is that of caring for tiny babies in multiple. Your babies may stay in the hospital neonatal intensive care unit (NICU) for a while. They will probably come home one at a time as they reach safe weights and develop sucking skills. They may come home with apnea and heart monitors in tow. (The apnea monitor provides assurance a child is breathing.)

Cribs. When your babies are very young, they won't be moving around much on their own. It's perfectly acceptable to put two or even three small babies in the same crib. We suggest you separate them when they are mature enough to wiggle around in the crib, preventing any baby from becoming a suffocation risk to another.

Diapers. As a prospective parent, you may have read exhaustive articles in newspapers and periodicals on the merits of disposable diapers versus cloth diapers. All combined, triplets will use between twenty-four and thirty diapers a day. So with multiples, the cost of diapers can become a significant item on the household budget. Weigh your options. For lowest cost up front, you would buy cloth diapers and wash them yourself. But when you factor in the need for daily loads of laundry, the cost in terms of time and inconvenience is considerable. Also, cloth can have a hidden cost built in due to increased incidence of diaper rash. And babies can't go as long between diaper changes in cloth as they can in disposable diapers, because of the lower absorbency of cloth diapers and their higher discomfort level when wet. Parents of multiples can find it hard enough to keep track of who has been changed and who is due for a fresh diaper—let alone be aware of who is wet or dirty at an *unexpected* time.

Disposable diapers are nice because babies don't experience discomfort even when a wet diaper is overlooked. On the other hand, commercial diaper services are cheaper than disposable diapers. But remember, you will have multiple quantities of wet, smelly diapers waiting for pickup each week. My personal preference is for disposable diapers but because of cost concerns, I encourage parents to try a diaper service and see if they can keep the babies changed and comfortable; if this service works for you, you may realize significant savings.

You Need Help

As I counsel parents of multiples, the single worst mistake I see them make is to assume they can handle this challenge on their own. Frequently, the budget is small and hired help is out of the question, so mom and dad set out to accomplish all child care duties on their own. Don't make this mistake! *You can't do it alone.*

You don't necessarily have to spend money to get help. There are several alternatives. Extended family members often love to help out—especially if your babies are eating and sleeping on a schedule.

Some high schools, colleges, seminaries, and yeshivas near your home may offer classes in childhood development. Your home could become a learning lab for a kind-hearted student. Churches and synagogues are filled with people available to lend a helping hand—you need only ask. If one or more of your children comes home using monitors, you may be a candidate for in-home nursing care at the state's expense. To find out about this possibility, check with the social worker associated with the neonatal intensive care unit of your hospital, or your pediatrician.

When someone asks if they can help, always say "Yes, please!" Keep a daily planner handy so you can give all who offer help an exact date and time they can serve you, right there on the spot; and immediately assign them a job. You may want help with baby care or, if your volunteers have limited time, ask them to help with your weekly errands—the laundry, post office, grocery store, pharmacy, and so on. *Delegating is one of the keys to preserving your sanity, with multiples.*

Let's Talk About Sleep

Sleeping for multiples is crucial to your peace of mind and to their happiness. With newborns—especially two or more small, premature babies—the temptation is to focus on how much they eat, how often they eat, and whether or not they are gaining weight consistently. My husband and I have applied the *Babywise* principles from birth on with our triplets, and we have counseled many parents of multiples to do the same. It has become clear that the true key to eating and weight gain is *sleep*. If you want your children to eat and to grow, then teach them to sleep. A rested baby will eat. An exhausted, agitated, sleep-deprived baby will howl, fuss, suck ineffectively, and spit up repeatedly.

You may be afraid your babies will wake up hungry an hour after you put them down if they have not taken a full feeding. The surprise is that they won't wake up hungry *before* the next feeding but will probably wake up *just in time* for the next scheduled feeding, better rested and ready to eat a full bottle. Overall, the newborn baby whose parents focus on sleep rather than on calories consumed will get more nutrition because he or she will be better rested, have better digestion, and be ready to suck strongly.

As your multiples mature, they will develop definite waketimes and sleep times. When they are newborn or premature, they will always fall asleep while you are feeding them, or maybe they won't even wake up for the feeding. As they get older, they will still get drowsy with feedings but with a little stimulation you can have them fully awake and ready to play after a meal. Waketime activities with multiples should always include some independent playtime. When the appointed time for the nap arrives, the babies may indicate readiness by being fussy and undistractable or they may be wide awake and cheery. *Put them down awake!* It will be clear that logistically you can't rock two, three, or more babies to sleep at each naptime. Your babies need to learn to comfort themselves. Multiple babies, even more than singletons, need to learn patience and how to calm themselves. The fact that mommy and daddy each have only one lap and one set of arms sets up some unavoidable limits. Self-comforting is particularly important when they are sick or under stress. If babies have learned the skill of sleep early on in life they will seek sleep

145

when they feel badly or tired, instead of further stressing themselves with crying and fussing.

If your multiple babies have been sharing a room since birth, they won't wake each other up. They will learn to shut out each other's crying, so don't separate them when one is fussing. When little ones are having a particularly hard cry, you can go in every ten minutes and pat them, reassure them, and possibly check for a wet or soiled diaper. You will function as a guide, teaching them how to self-comfort. Go in to them only long enough to cause them to stop crying but not long enough for them to fall asleep. Your goal is to put them down awake, allowing them to fall asleep on their own—without a transition process, such as rocking or patting. This can be more challenging than it sounds, due to the sheer physical effort of caring for multiples.

You need to start and finish each eat/wake/sleep cycle in a fairly structured fashion. It takes about fifteen to twenty minutes to pick up three babies, diaper them, and put them in their cribs for a nap. One common pitfall for parents is to allow their babies to fall asleep in their waketime activity chairs or swings. Parents get busy doing a household chore, answering the phone, or trying to solve one baby's problem, only to find the others have fallen asleep sitting up. While it's true they've fallen asleep by themselves, they didn't do this in the *right place*—their own cribs. If this happens often, they may develop difficulty self-comforting as they lay in their cribs. There will always be unexpected events to contend with, but try to plan ahead by putting your babies down awake in their cribs when you are not distracted. That way, when they do fall asleep sitting up, it will be a rare event and not a habit.

As they continue to mature, a brand-new problem arises: Between six and nine months of age, your babies will discover each other. This is where the party really begins! Now your problem is that they are having too much fun entertaining each other. They won't wake up to each other's crying but *will* wake up to each other's laughter and carrying on. They have built-in buddies. What helps in this situation is to have a toy that can be played with quietly in bed while a baby's siblings continue to sleep. In our family we used "Busy Box"-type activity toys. Other families place small, noiseless toys in each child's bed after the children have fallen asleep, so the baby who wakes up can play quietly and independently with the toy.

Strongly discourage your multiples from getting out of their cribs on their own. All babies should stay in their cribs until given permission but for multiples there is an additional safety issue—the threat one aggressive toddler poses to another when unsupervised. We convinced our triplets that climbing in and out of their cribs was impossible without the help of a step ladder. When the step ladder was not available, they didn't get in and out of their cribs. They slept in their cribs until after their third birthday, without any episodes of unauthorized entry or exit.

Let's Talk about Feeding

Are you going to breast feed? A mother of multiples often *can* breast feed. Whether this is the right choice for you and your babies is entirely up to you and your children to determine. Much will depend on: your babies' maturity at birth and whether or not they require NICU care; whether or not you had a cesarean section; and how many babies you have. Mothers of twins are more successful at breast feeding than mothers of triplets. If your babies come right home with you from the hospital, it will be much easier to establish a breast-feeding pattern.

As explained in chapter five, a mother's milk is a complete and perfect food. It is easily digested, provides excellent nutrition, and contains the right balance of proteins and fats. It also provides additional antibodies that are necessary for establishing your baby's early immune system. If your babies are in the NICU, even if you don't plan to breast feed them directly, you may want to provide milk for them using an electric breast pump. Many pediatricians recommend this and insurance companies will often reimburse a mother for the pump rental while the baby is in the NICU. Premature babies are especially in need of their mother's antibodies that are provided in breast milk.

Each of your babies is different. You may plan to breast feed all of them but find that one prefers the bottle to the breast. Some moms successfully breast feed all of their multiples in a rotating fashion, with one baby receiving a bottle each feeding while the others have a turn at the breast. Other mothers produce enough milk to feed all three of their triplets. A good electric pump is very helpful in establishing and maintaining a milk supply for multiples. You may be able to pump after you feed one or two babies so that a third baby can receive breast milk in a bottle. I haven't yet heard of quadruplets being successfully breast fed. Breast feeding can be magnificently easy once established and learned by mom and babies, but it doesn't start out easy, especially after the stress of a high-risk pregnancy. Please relax your expectations of yourself and get good counsel from a professional lactation consultant. Breast feeding a multiple birth may not come naturally and you probably will need some counsel.

If your newborn babies are low birth-weight and/or premature, they will probably sleep all the time. You may find they hardly ever wake up, sleeping even when you are changing their diapers, bathing them, and feeding them. Premature babies react unexpectedly to stimulus by withdrawing and sleeping. Don't fight their sleepiness. Do your best to get the food into them but don't try for more than thirty minutes every three hours. By this I mean that from the beginning of one feeding to the beginning of the next, no more than three hours should elapse. Attempt to feed and burp each infant for thirty minutes, putting the sleeping baby back to bed for the remaining two and a half hours of the cycle. Do this even if the baby was sucking ineffectively and only received a fraction of the usual feeding amount, or when a significant amount of the feeding is spit back up. I recommend that you don't refeed after a baby spits up if the thirty-minute limit is up. If the baby spits up ten minutes or so into the feeding, try refeeding until the time is up.

One important aspect of feeding newborn and premature infants is a good assessment of their hydration. *Each baby should have between six and eight wet diapers each day.* If you are breast feeding, this will be one clue to help you determine that they are properly latched on and consuming adequate quantities of milk. But with a multiple birth, especially three or more babies, keeping track of who has had a wet diaper and who hasn't can become a challenge. Especially in the first sleep-deprived postpartum weeks, you can lose track of even obvious things. So write it all down. Keep your "Healthy Baby Growth Charts" near the changing table and keep them updated. Consider color coding it, assigning a different color to each child. This will make it easier to keep track of each child's progress.

As your babies mature, feedings will become easier and you will probably be able to feed each baby in under thirty minutes. Adhere closely to the feeding time/waketime/naptime order for each baby. When one wakes at night to eat, wake them all and feed them. However, when one wakes up early from a nap, resist the temptation to reward the baby with a feeding. Instead, check for a dirty diaper, calm the baby, and lead the child into comforting himself or herself and going back to sleep.

Routine for Multiples

The routine of each baby shouldn't vary but the eat/sleep schedule of your multiple-birth babies, *with respect to one another*, may be impacted by many factors. How many babies are there? How many feeders are there? Are you breast feeding? Each baby should have feeding time, waketime, and naptime. Don't change that order, except for late-night feedings when there is no waketime, and for premature babies who aren't neurologically mature enough to tolerate waketime.

If you have triplets and there is only one caregiver for them most of the time, you may choose to stagger your babies' schedules. Here's how this might work: The feeder (probably you) starts the process on the hour with baby A, finishes half an hour later and goes on to baby B, while baby A has waketime in a bouncy seat nearby. At the top of the next hour, baby C wakes for feeding and baby A is ready for naptime. When all three babies are fed there is an hour and a half of nonfeeding time before the cycle starts again. If there are two feeders in your home, you could always have two babies eating at the same time.

With more help, all babies in a home with triplets or twins can be on approximately the same schedule. With two helpers, three babies can eat at the same time. Because babies eat at different speeds, there will be a fast eater and a slow eater. Once you figure out who eats slowest and who fastest, you can establish a system whereby one helper feeds the slow eater while the second helper feeds the fastest eater and the in-between eater. A breast-feeding mom can feed two babies at the same time while someone gives a bottle to the third baby.

Older bottle-fed babies can be propped up and fed two at a time or even three at a time, but you can't prop up bottles for premature babies or small babies who are having difficulty learning to suck.

Waketime

You won't need to focus on waketime during the first weeks your babies are home, but soon they will stay awake for the whole feeding and begin to take an interest in the world around them. A reclining upright seat is the perfect place to put a baby for these early waketime periods. The seat allows the baby to look around and wave arms and legs while still upright, while at the same time discouraging them from spiting up—a common occurrence in babies who are lying horizontally. Reclining seats are useful later for feeding a propped-up bottle or for beginning solids when the babies are still too small for highchairs. A word of caution: *Never leave a baby unattended in a seat.*

Waketime activity for multiples doesn't require that you have three of everything. Babies tire of most activities after ten to twenty minutes, so you can set up rotating "stations." One baby is in the windup swing while another plays with a rattle in the playpen; the third is in the bouncy seat playing with a different rattle or sitting with mommy singing a song and playing one-on-one. At fifteen-minute intervals, you rotate the babies to the next activity.

Individual time is essential to happy multiples. They need independent play time each day, and they also need individual, one-on-one time with mommy and daddy. By necessity we tend to think of multiples as a unit. We feed, change, dress, and bathe them all at the same time. It's much easier to make sure you are being fair and that everyone's needs are being met if you keep the babies on a schedule and do all major daily activities collectively. How you structure waketime and the way you plan the babies' play activities can offer a break from the monotony of cookie-cutter baby care. Leave all but one of the babies with your spouse or a helper and take just one for a walk or on an errand to the store. Or read just one a story while the others play independently.

As multiples enter toddlerhood, they find themselves in a world where there is always someone else their size grabbing at them or at the toy they are about to pick up. Time in a playpen for a multiple becomes a time of refuge. They can do whatever they want there without someone interrupting them and taking their things. You can have one of nearly every other piece of equipment, but multiple playpens—one for each child—is a good early investment. Playpen time also provides a welcome relief for mommy: she can answer the phone or make lunch while the children play safely. Begin to practice

playpen time at three to four months of age. Start with just ten minutes a day and slowly increase the time, so that by one year of age,
they can stay in the playpen for at least forty minutes.

A Word to Husbands

The key to harmonious family life is the primacy of the husband-
wife relationship. All other relationships in the home are impacted—
positively or negatively—by the health and success of the husband-
wife relationship. You will only be as good a parent as you are a
spouse. For this reason, it's even more essential with multiples that
dad help out. Your wife will only be able to listen to, share, and enjoy
you if she feels your support and encouragement. Your wife is the
chief feeder, diaper-changer, bather, and entertainer of a multiple
birth. She has no "down time." Twenty-four hours a day she has to
be calm and controlled, so she can make the important assessments
and decisions that are part of the babies' daily life. The more you
cherish and serve her, the more you will get back in the form of a
composed, wise mom and peaceful, secure children.

Chapter Eleven

Parenting Potpourri:

Topics of Interest to New Parents

*I*f you are a new or prospective parent, you probably are seeking answers to a variety of baby-related questions. In this chapter we address some topics that are likely to be of interest to you; they are arranged in alphabetical order for easy reference. (Much of this material is dealt with more extensively in *BABYWISE II*; you can get more information about *BABYWISE II* at the end of this book.)

Achievement Levels

Much has been written regarding what an infant is supposed to be doing physically during his or her first year of life. This includes mastering such tasks as shaking a rattle, saying "da da," reaching for bright objects, and crawling. There are three important things to remember here. *First*, a baby's basic routine enhances learning. Order is an ally of the learning process. *Second*, infants will differ in the age at which they master skills. There is no cause for alarm if your child seems to develop skills more slowly than you believe he or she should, nor should you compare your child's development with your neighbor's child. *Third*, along with his or her physical development, your baby will become more and more responsive to moral training. Be careful not to focus solely on your baby's physical accomplishments, without giving due consideration to his or her developing attitudes.

Baby Blues

Postpartum depression is commonly referred to as "baby blues," and is now receiving significant attention from the media. Physically, there is a hormonal change that takes place in a mother right after delivery. For some women, it takes longer for those hormones to be brought back into balance.

Although some women find themselves depressed and weepy several days after giving birth, not all women experience postpartum depression. Many who do have certain traits in common—they're not on a routine, they nurse frequently, and they are up several times during the night—all of which leave them in a perpetual state of exhaustion. Each of these symptoms can be traced back to the strain that lack of routine puts on a mother. You can greatly minimize the symptoms of postpartum depression by keeping yourself on a good routine, getting plenty of rest, and watching your diet. If you find that after several weeks you are still abnormally melancholy, talk to your obstetrician.

Baby Equipment

One thing to remember about baby equipment is that much of it is optional. (However, a car seat is an absolute necessity if your baby is ever to travel by car or truck!) You don't need to follow all the recommended baby equipment lists that appear in parenting magazines or in baby stores. Your baby isn't going to know or care if he or she has coordinating furniture, so don't worry if that isn't in your budget. There are some items—beyond the usual high chair, stroller, changing table, and crib—that would be helpful, and you often can borrow them or purchase them at a garage sale.

Baby Monitor

The monitor can serve a useful purpose by allowing you to hear your baby if you happen to have a large home or are working outdoors during your baby's nap. There is no need to keep it by your bedside at night. You *will* hear your baby cry during those hours. During the still of the night, the monitor magnifies every sound your baby makes, robbing you of needed sleep. The last thing your child needs in the morning is a cranky parent.

Car Seat

A car seat should be functional, not only for your infant but also for your toddler. Think long term when you make this investment. Some car seats are very stylish and work fine for your infant but may not be practical for a growing toddler, thus necessitating the purchase of a second car seat. An infant younger than six months does not have strong neck muscles, so prevent his or her head from rolling from side to side while driving. This can be accomplished by rolling cloth diapers or receiving blankets and using these to support each side of your baby's head.

Crib

Cribs, cradles, and cots are not products of the industrial revolution, as some might guess. They have been used by parents for millennia. For example, three ancient Mediterranean societies (Greek, Roman, and Hebrew) all used cribs for their babies.

The cradle, which is an infant crib with rocking motion, gained popularity in the Middle Ages. Eventually it became a status symbol of wealth. The use of cribs and cradles has not been limited to Europe or the Mediterranean basin. Mothers in primitive settings even today hang cribs from the ceiling of their huts, where they can gently rock their babies as they pass by. For twentieth-century parents, the crib is one of the most basic pieces of baby furniture they will own. Give thought to the one you will buy or borrow. After all, nearly half of your child's existence for the first eighteen months of life will be spent in it.

When deciding on a crib, look for certain features. The mattress should fit snugly against all four sides, and it should be firm and of good quality. A snug fit prevents the baby from getting any of his body parts stuck between the mattress and the slats. The guardrail should be at least twenty-six inches above the top of the mattress. This will discourage any attempt to climb out when the baby is older. The spaces between the crib slats should be no more than two-and-three-eighths inches apart. A crib bumper-guard is a good investment and is safer for the baby than using pillows or stuffed animals. The latter should be kept out of the newborn's crib because of the potential danger of suffocation.

The location of the crib in the room is another consideration. Avoid placing the crib near drafty windows, heaters, or hot air ducts. A steady blast of hot air can dry out your baby's nose and throat, leading to respiratory problems.

Infant Seat

You will use the infant seat from day one and use it more than any other piece of equipment in the early weeks and months. When your child is old enough to be spoon fed, an infant seat is preferable to a high chair, since at this age the child does not have the strength to sit up. Please note: *The infant seat is not a car seat.*

Infant Sling

In some third-world nations, mothers carry their babies in an infant sling as they move through their day. For these mothers it is simply a matter of convenience, because where they go, the baby must go. In our society, such a practice is not necessary. There is a place and time for backpacks, snugglies, and slings, such as when mom, dad, and their baby are out shopping, hiking, or taking a walk. But slinging your baby at your side all day long is an artificial way to parent. You are not a marsupial, and your baby should not be treated like a kangaroo joey!

If you use a sling, do so thoughtfully. In our opinion, much more developmental damage is done to a child by holding him or her constantly than by putting the baby down. The child needs to learn to explore life on his or her own and should be given opportunities to grow in independence. Although slinging your baby all day long makes perfect sense to those who embrace the birth-trauma theory (a theory which we reject), for the rest of us, the practice of slinging is a concern. In terms of biomechanics alone, carrying a baby in a sling can increase neck and back problems, or even create them.

Playpen

Once parents have their infant's eating and sleeping patterns under control, it's time to do the same with waketime activities. This goal is best accomplished by using the playpen, an invaluable piece of equipment. During the 1970s, playpens were dismissed as a hindrance to a child's natural development. Today, researchers know better. Playpens are necessary to help parents optimize their child's development. Here are some of the benefits of using a playpen.

1. *It provides a safe environment.* Playpens are a safe environment for an infant when mom's attention must be elsewhere and it's not the baby's naptime. Mom can take a shower or unload the groceries from the car, care for other children, and do a host of other activities, knowing her baby is safe.

2. *It doubles as a portable bed.* The playpen can be a portable bed. Especially useful when visiting another home, the playpen gives the baby a clean and familiar place to sleep.

3. *It offers a structured learning center.* Most importantly, your baby's first structured learning takes place in the playpen. The partnership a child has with the playpen helps establish foundational intellectual skills. Planned daily, playpen times allow a little one the opportunity to develop:

a) Mental focusing skills. (The ability to concentrate on an object or activity at hand and not be constantly distracted.)

b) A sustained attention span.

c) Creativity. (Creativity is the product of boundaries, not freedom. With absolute freedom, there is no need for creative thinking or problem-solving.)

d) The ability to entertain himself or herself.

e) Orderliness.

These skills could be seriously delayed if your child misses out on structured playpen time.

Parents can begin using the playpen as a safe environment or as a portable bed soon after the baby is born. Playpen time (using the playpen as a learning center) may begin as soon as the baby has alert waketimes of fifteen to thirty minutes. At least one of those waketimes each day can be spent in the playpen. By two months of age, the playpen should be a well-established part of your baby's routine.

Start by putting your baby in the playpen for fifteen minutes once or twice a day. Select times when the baby is fresh and alert (not right before naptime). Put several interesting toys within your baby's reach, or use a crib gym or a mobile. Local libraries carry books that will describe the types of toys or activities your baby is likely to be interested in at each stage of development.

Bathing Your Baby

Your baby should not receive his or her first full bath until the remainder of the umbilical cord has fallen off (seven to fourteen days after birth). Never interfere with the natural process of the cord falling off. After it does, you are free to bathe your baby in either a special tub or on a towel placed in the kitchen sink.

Always monitor the water temperature. Don't base the temperature solely on what feels right to you, but on what seems comfortable to your baby. An infant doesn't need to receive a full bath every day—a sponge bath some days is sufficient. Soap doesn't need to be used every day, either; overuse may dry your baby's skin. The most important bath-related advice we can give you is this: *Never leave your baby alone in water.* Adhering to this rule without fail can prevent tragedy.

Bonding with Your Baby

The concept of parent-child bonding, once a precise academic theory, has evolved into one of general application to the parent-child relationship. The theory concerns itself with ensuring that a new mother does not reject her offspring.

Some have asserted that the first minutes or hours after birth constitute a sensitive period during which a mother should have close physical contact with her newborn. This theory supposes that a mother would instinctively be drawn closer to her child in the future if bonding (brought about by face-to-face and skin-to-skin contact) takes place soon after birth. This supposedly gives an advantage to the child and will help him or her reach optimal potential. If only parenthood were that easy!

While maternal-infant bonding is an interesting psychological idea, research has not substantiated the cause-and-effect relationship this theory speaks of, in human beings. And although nonrational animals show some instinctive tendency of this sort, speculating that rational man responds similarly is scientifically unacceptable. Anthropology—the study of mankind—is very different from zoology, the study of animals.[1]

There is nothing wrong with a newborn cuddling with his or her mother right after birth or having a close time together with his or her new family. If it's possible, we encourage you to do that. Take time to acknowledge the wonderful creation of a new life. But don't think those first minutes are more binding or important than all the hours and days that will follow. Building a healthy parent-child relationship doesn't take place in a moment of time; it's a long-term process.

Cesarean Birth

The purpose for cesarean section surgery is basic: to safeguard the life of the baby or the mother. Most often referred to as a *c-section*, delivery is accomplished through an incision in the abdominal wall and uterus. The decision to do a c-section may be made either prior to your due date because of a known condition or because of an unexpected complication during labor. In either case, competent doctors have your best interests in mind.

More unnecessary c-sections are performed today than in years past. There are two primary reasons for this fact. First, we have developed greater technology for saving babies. Second, there are more lawsuits against obstetricians and gynecologists today, forcing them to exercise conservative, lower-risk treatment. Keep in mind that having a c-section performed is a medical decision that in no way reflects on your motherhood. There is no need to feel guilty or embarrassed over it. Just be thankful you and your baby are healthy.

Church Nurseries and Baby-Sitters

Nursery workers and baby-sitters provide a wonderful service. Unfortunately, some moms and dads demand that the nursery workers keep their babies on a rigid routine. Parents should be gracious and appreciative when leaving a child in the nursery or in other special baby-sitting situations. Nursery workers aren't obligated to maintain your baby's schedule because there is no way they can keep track of ten, fifteen, or twenty different schedules.

When your baby goes to the nursery, leave a bottle of water, formula, or breast milk and give the nursery worker the freedom to do what he or she thinks is best. It won't harm your baby's routine to be fed earlier than what is scheduled this time. You will be able to return to your baby's normal routine later in the day.

We are encouraged by the fact that so many parents understand the value of order in their lives and their children's lives. But sometimes people redefine order to mean rigidity, and that leads to imbalance. Balance includes both structure and flexibility.

Circumcision

Circumcision is almost as old as history itself. The practice was historically (though not exclusively) a Jewish rite. Today, medical experts and studies tend to agree on the value of circumcision, although not all agree on the necessity of it. Evidence suggests that circumcision may decrease the risk of urinary tract infection and that it virtually eliminates the possibility of cancer of the penis. Parents should also consider the social ramifications of circumcision. How will your son feel in a locker room full of other boys during his school years?

For the infant, circumcision is not the traumatic experience that some portray. His minor surgery and any discomfort felt will not be rooted in his memory any more than will his being pricked with a heel stick during his PKU blood test soon after birth.

Crib Death

The unexpected death of a seemingly healthy baby is referred to as Sudden Infant Death Syndrome (SIDS), or crib death. What do we know about SIDS? We know it's responsible for seven thousand deaths a year and is neither predictable nor preventable. There are more male victims, especially among those who are born prematurely, and it occurs more often among babies of minorities, young single mothers, and those who smoke.

A child can be victimized by SIDS anytime during the first year, with the highest percentage of these deaths occurring between the second and fourth months. More babies die of SIDS in the winter months than in summer, and more in colder climates than in warmer ones.

Some family-bed advocates suggest that sleeping with your baby can decrease the possibility of SIDS. This conclusion is drawn from data compiled in third-world nations, where fewer SIDS cases were reported among children who slept with their parents, compared to SIDS cases in North America. Their conclusion ignores some very important information which we need to share with you. First, most third-world nations are found in warmer climates, where SIDS frequency would be expected to be four to five times less, due to the absence of cold weather. And second, when a comparison is made *within* a third-world society, families with parents who sleep with their children have equal or higher rates of infant deaths than those who don't sleep with their children.

Some researchers suggest that putting a baby on his or her back for sleep, rather than on the baby's tummy, will reduce the chance of crib death. That research is not conclusive, and the method of gathering supportive data is questionable. To state that babies in Nigeria have a lower SIDS rate than American babies because they're put down on their backs is entirely too simplistic, with many variables left unaccounted for. We suggest you speak to your health-care provider about any questions you have concerning SIDS and the positioning of your baby. Rare as it may be, parents should be concerned with the possibility their baby could aspirate vomit (breathe it into the lungs) when an abnormally high amount of it erupts with no place to go—if the baby is lying on his or her back. When on his or her tummy or side, gravity will prevent any vomit from entering a baby's respiratory system.

One last word about crib death. The one thing that most pediatricians agree upon is the need for a firm mattress of good quality. Soft mattresses with questionable stuffing material should be avoided. Spend the extra money required for a good mattress.

Diapers

As new parents, you have a choice between disposable or cloth diapers. It really is a matter of personal preference. As a general rule, you will change your baby's diaper at each feeding. For demand-fed babies, that could be as many as twelve diapers a day. PDF babies average six to seven diaper changes a day, coinciding with their feedings.

At the nighttime feeding it is not necessary to change your baby's diaper, with the exception of one that is soaked or soiled. Remember, your goal is for your baby to sleep through the night, not to wake up for a diaper change. When your baby begins to sleep through the night, use a medium diaper. They will seem larger only because today's babies are not expected to sleep through the night as early as those on PDF.

Diaper Rash

A diaper rash may be caused by yeast infections, food allergies, new teeth, or sitting too long in a messy diaper. If your baby has sensitive skin, he or she may be more prone to diaper rash. Have your pediatrician recommend an over-the-counter medication for minor irritations, or a prescription medication for more severe problems.

Grandparents

There is a special relationship between the third generation and the first. Take advantage of every opportunity for a grandparent to enjoy your child, within reason. Don't assume your parents want to baby-sit, or abuse their generous offer to do so. And don't surrender your parenting responsibilities to your parents. While they may very much enjoy their grandchildren, they are not the parents—you are.

Many grandparents travel a great distance to visit soon after the baby is born. That visit can either be a blessing or a problem, depending on your relationship and just how like-minded you are. You may want to ask the traveling grandparents to visit ten days to two weeks after the baby is born. By then you will have worked through your basic parenting approach and will feel somewhat comfortable with what you are doing. Having a high-powered, take-charge relative come in right after birth can be very hard on a new mother's emotions. A husband can help by protecting his wife from unwelcome intrusions.

Growth Spurts

Growth spurts for your infant will probably begin at around four to six weeks of age and will likely occur approximately every three or four weeks after that in the early months of the baby's life. If your baby has been content after feedings but suddenly no longer is, he or she probably is beginning a growth spurt. The nursing mom may find the baby wanting to nurse longer, and there will be some frustration on baby's part if the mother doesn't have enough milk. If you are breast-feeding, these spurts may necessitate an extra feeding for a couple of days to increase your milk supply for your baby's increased demand. If you are feeding approximately every four hours when this happens, drop back to three hours a couple of times a day. If you are bottle-feeding and suspect your baby is experiencing a growth spurt, simply offer more formula per feeding. However, beware of using growth spurts as an excuse for prolonged extra feedings; return to your baby's routine as soon as possible.

Immunization

The ability to protect our children from the tragedies of polio, smallpox, and other deadly diseases is one of the advantages of our day. Medical research has provided us with effective immunizations which build up antibodies to fight off invading diseases. But the vaccines are useless if a child never receives them. Although the legitimacy of some vaccines is in question, parents are responsible to see that their children are fully protected.

The common vaccinations offered are polio, diphtheria, hepatitis B, pertussis (whooping cough), tetanus, rubella (German measles), mumps, measles, and *Hemophilus influenza*, type b (Hib). With the exception of the hepatitis B vaccination, which usually is administered before the newborn baby is discharged from the hospital, most pediatricians start routine immunizations when a baby is two months old.

Immunization Schedule

DTP	2 months, 4 months, 6 months, 15–18 months, and 4–6 years
Polio	2 months, 4 months, 6 months, and 4–6 years
Hepatitis B	at birth, 1–2 months, 6–18 months
Hib	2 months, 4 months, 6 months, 12–15 months
TB	Test for at 12 months
Measles	12–15 months, 4–6 years
Mumps	12–15 months, 4–6 years
Rubella	12–15 months, 4–6 years
Tetanus	14–16 years
Diphtheria	14–16 years

(Note: *DTP* in the schedule above refers to diphtheria, tetanus, and pertussis; *TB* refers to the vaccination against tuberculosis; the vaccination for measles, mumps, and rubella is commonly referred to as an *MMR*.)

Immunization schedules change frequently as better vaccines and more information become available. Ask your pediatrician to give you a current vaccination schedule.

Jaundice in Newborns

Newborn jaundice is a medical condition, not a disease. It's characterized by a yellow tinge to the skin and eyes, caused by the pigment *bilirubin* in the blood. A mild degree of jaundice is common in most newborns. If it appears to be more pronounced after the second day, frequent blood tests are performed and conservative treatment initiated.

Part of that treatment includes an increase in fluid intake. You don't necessarily have to nurse more often. Sticking with a strict two-and-a-half-hour feeding routine is normally sufficient to bring down the bilirubin levels. Supplementary liquids may be recommended by your pediatrician. In addition, babies with moderately raised levels of bilirubin are treated with special fluorescent lights that help to break down the yellow pigment. Your doctor will determine the program of treatment that is right for your baby. Because a newborn with jaundice will tend to sleep more, make sure you wake your baby and feed him or her at least every three hours. Jaundice is usually easily controlled, but it could develop into a dangerous situation when ignored or left untreated.

The Microwave and the Bottle

Occasionally you may want to heat your baby's bottle in a microwave oven. That can be dangerous unless certain precautions are taken. Microwaves heat foods unevenly, so be sure to shake the bottle well after heating and squirt a dab of milk on your wrist to test for warmth. Unlike formula, breast milk can be destroyed in the heating process if care is not taken. When heating your baby's bottle, be sure to loosen the top to allow for heat expansion; otherwise, it may explode.

Nursing Twins

For a mother to nurse twins successfully, the PDF plan is a must. Assign a breast to each twin and keep them nursing that specified breast throughout all feedings. This will help the supply to keep up with the unique demand of each twin. Let one twin set the pace, and keep them both on that schedule. If this means you must wake one, do so. If this means one must cry before his or her feeding, this is acceptable too; you are not being cruel to the child.

Right after they are born, you can nurse them simultaneously, using a football hold—your arms are bent to support the back of each baby while each head rests on a breast. As they grow, your babies will have to nurse one at a time. Beyond that distinction, you will be able to implement all other aspects of the parent-directed feeding plan, including feeding routines and sleeping through the night. May you thoroughly enjoy your "double portion"! (For a more complete discussion of how to deal with a multiple birth, see Chapter 10, "Multiple Birth: The Endless Party.")

Pacifiers and Thumb-Sucking

Breast-feeding mothers should not let themselves be used as pacifiers. Some infants have a need to suck a little longer after feeding time. An actual pacifier is very useful for them. That is especially true of infants who nurse so efficiently that feeding time lasts a total of only five to ten minutes. Pacifiers can also be used to extend the time between feedings, when a baby is fussy but not hungry. However, be careful not to use the pacifier as a "plug" whenever your baby fusses. Don't create habits that will have to be broken later.

Some children will not take a pacifier but find their thumb instead. That's fine. Consider how long you will use the pacifier or allow your child to suck his or her thumb. If thumb-sucking persists past two years, limit it to the child's bedroom. That boundary will help you eliminate the practice later on.

Sleeping with Your Baby

It is common for children in third-world countries to sleep in the same bed with their parents. In most cases this is done for pragmatic reasons: There is only one bed and often only one room. Poverty forces the sleeping arrangement, not the pursuit of psychological health for the child. For modern America, the family bed finds its roots in the birth-trauma theory. As stated previously, the practice allows for the constant presence of the mother, as required by the theory's hypothesis.

The family bed is unsafe. The Consumer Protection Safety Commission warns parents against sleeping with their infants because of the death hazard. They are joined by the vast majority of health care professionals in America, who agree the practice is dangerous. The child could smother beneath a sleeping adult, become wedged between the mattress or against an adjacent wall, or suffocate face down, especially on a waterbed. These terrible things do happen. There is not a single benefit gained that can possibly outweigh the risk.

Some *countries* discourage the practice. New Zealand, for example, has cut down on infant death dramatically by educating young parents to the dangers of sleeping with a baby. As more infant deaths are reported in America, state legislators are beginning to consider laws designed to discourage the practice. Why take a chance?

Sleeping with your baby creates needs but doesn't fulfill them. Your child won't be any more secure, feel more loved, or have any greater advantages in life than a child who sleeps alone. What the nighttime parenting advocates gloss over are sleep problems created as the child grows older. We believe this practice hinders the development of trust between parent and child, since the child is never given the opportunity to learn how to trust. The child who can sleep alone, knowing that mom and dad will come when truly needed, is much more secure than the child who is never alone and can't exist outside his or her parents' presence. With the latter, trust is based upon proximity rather than a relationship. The measure of a child's security is never found in the presence of his or her parent, but in how well the child copes away from parents. The benefits of shared sleep are clearly exaggerated.

Shared sleep confuses infant sleep cycles. And separation anxiety often occurs when the child is asked to leave mom and dad's bed. If an infant is placed in his or her own bed and room right from the beginning, no separation anxiety takes place since no dependent nighttime relationship is established. Also, shared sleep has proven problematic for many nursing mothers, since the fear of rolling on top of the baby creates anxiety which affects sleep and milk production.

Contrast the nighttime peace associated with a baby sleeping soundly in his or her crib to the squeezed, squirming, and disrupted sleep moms and dads who share a bed with their baby experience. As one mother states, in reference to having her baby sleep with her and her husband, "It wasn't as natural as they said it would be. Every sound, move, and restless fit the child made was amplified. We held our breath hoping upon hope that the child would not wake and demand of me. My comfort during the day and night became a reluctant duty and not a true expression of a mother's love. The theory robbed me of the joy of motherhood."

There is nothing wrong with a child taking a nap with mom or dad once in a while, or with cuddling the baby in bed before everyone gets up. But patterns you establish in the first couple of days, weeks, and months, whether right or wrong, will become those to which your little one will adjust. The longer wrong patterns persist, the harder they will be to break.

Spitting Up

This is a common event in the life of every infant. At first it may be frightening to a new parent, but it is normal and not a cause for alarm. Proper burping during and after feeding can minimize and sometimes eliminate the problem. (For a discussion of how to burp your baby, see the material near the end of Chapter 5, headed "Burping Your Baby.") Your baby may have taken in more milk than he or she needed. Refeeding is not usually necessary. Keep in mind that babies vary tremendously; some rarely spit up, while others spit up all the time. If your child is growing, gaining weight, and is happy and healthy, then he or she is fine.

Projectile vomiting is not the same thing as spitting up. Instead of bringing back up just part of his or her meal, the baby powerfully ejects the entire contents of the stomach. If your baby experiences this type of vomiting routinely, call your pediatrician.

Starting Solid Foods

Parent-directed feeding continues with the addition of solids (baby food and table foods) to your baby's menu. Add solids at existing family mealtimes, working toward three meals a day. With the production of saliva at about three months of age, you will see the baby preparing for a change in menu (although you will not begin feeding your child solids until he or she is four to six months of age).

In your child's first year, the calories he or she gains from liquids (breast milk or formula) are of primary importance. During the second half of the first year, a gradual transition occurs. Though your baby may still drink as much at twelve months as at six months, he or she will need more and more calories from solids.

Generally, you should start adding solids to your baby's diet at between four and six months, depending on the baby's weight gain and sleep patterns. Your pediatrician will advise you. The first food to add to your baby's meals is rice cereal. Later, you will add other single-grain cereals. Specific information about adding solids to your baby's diet are discussed in *BABYWISE II*.

Teething

When a tooth begins to break through the gum, a baby experiences the condition commonly referred to as *teething*. Like jaundice, teething isn't a disease; it's a condition of growth. Your baby's first teeth will push through at between six and eight months of age. By six months, one baby out of three has one tooth, and by nine months, the typical baby has three teeth. The natural process of teething should not interfere with breast-feeding, since the sucking is done by the tongue and palate, not by the gums.

Irritability, fussiness, increased salivation, and a slightly raised temperature sometimes accompany new teeth. As uncomfortable as these symptoms may be, teething is not a catch-all excuse for chronic poor behavior or a drastic change in your baby's routine.

Weaning Your Baby

Weaning, by today's definition, is the process by which parents offer food supplements in place of, or in addition to, mother's milk. That process begins the moment parents offer a bottle of formula or when their baby first tastes cereal. From that moment on, weaning is generally a gradual process.

From the Breast

The duration of breast-feeding has varied from the extremes of birth to fifteen years. No one can say for sure at what age weaning should take place. For some it may be six months, for others a year. Breast-feeding for more than a year is a matter of preference, since adequate supplementary food is usually available. Several thousand years ago, weaning took place at between eighteen and twenty-four months of age. A baby being nursed as long as three years was rare.

At birth, infants are totally dependent on their caregiver to meet their physical needs. But they must gradually become more independent, in small increments. One step toward independence for your baby is the ability to feed himself or herself. You can start this process by eliminating one feeding at a time, going three to four days before dropping the next one. That time frame allows your body to make the proper adjustments in milk reduction.

Usually the late-afternoon feeding is the easiest one to drop, since it is a busy time of day. Replace each feeding with six to eight ounces of formula or milk (depending on the child's age). Pediatricians generally recommend that parents not give their babies cow's milk until they are at least one year of age. If your baby is nine months or older, consider going straight to a cup rather than to a bottle. The transition will be easiest if you have introduced the cup prior to weaning.

From the Bottle

When your baby is one year of age, you can begin to wean him or her from the bottle. Some mothers wean straight to a cup with great success. Although an infant can become very attached to a bottle, you can minimize that problem by not letting your child hold it for extended periods of time. There is a difference between playing with the bottle and drinking from it. The weaning process takes time, so be prepared to be patient. Begin by eliminating the bottle at one meal, then at another, and so on.

Chapter Twelve

Newborn Q & A

*T*his chapter is made up of questions new or prospective mothers have asked, along with our answers to those questions. You probably will find that some of your own concerns and parenting experiences are similar to those expressed in these questions.

1. When my baby is brought to me for his very first feeding, how long should I let him nurse?

If possible, nurse your baby soon after birth (within the first hour-and-a-half), since that is when newborns are usually most alert. We suggest you strive for fifteen minutes per side (with a minimum of no less than ten minutes per side), remembering the importance of positioning the baby properly on the breast. If your baby wants to nurse longer during this first feeding, allow him to do so. In fact, with the first several feedings, you can go as long as the two of you are comfortable. Both breasts need to be stimulated at each feeding, and the initial time frame mentioned above will allow for sufficient breast stimulation.

Over the course of the next three to five days, create and maintain your basic two-and-a-half- to three-hour routine, nursing fifteen to twenty minutes per side. This means your average nursing period falls to between twenty and thirty minutes per feeding during this first week.

2. *I've just brought my newborn home from the hospital. She likes to sleep from 10:00 A.M. until 3:00 P.M., and eat every three hours the rest of the day and night. Is this routine acceptable?*

No. Your baby has her nights and days mixed up. Parent-directed feeding offers a proactive management plan for your baby. Wake your baby and feed her at three-hour intervals during the day. In a few days, she will get her days and nights lined up with the rest of the family.

3. *My two-week-old daughter nurses on one side, then falls asleep. Two hours later, she wants to eat again. What should I do?*

You need to keep your baby awake during feeding time and teach her to nurse from both sides equally. Try changing her diaper between sides, undressing her, and rubbing her head, feet, or nose. Do what you must to keep her awake and finish the task at hand— which is eating. Babies learn very quickly from the laws of natural consequences. If your daughter doesn't eat at one feeding, then make her wait until the next one. That will probably only happen once. Don't feed her between routine mealtimes; otherwise, you are teaching her to snack, not eat.

4. *My baby starts to cry two hours after most of his feedings, and seems to be hungry each time. I've tried to stretch it beyond this two hours, but can't get him to go longer. What's the problem?*

The most common reason a baby fails to make the two-and-a-half-hour minimum (especially babies under two weeks of age) is that the order of daytime activities has been reversed. The events must follow in this order: feeding time, waketime, then naptime. When a baby goes only two hours between feedings, it's usually due to the reversal of the last two activities. After the feeding time, try to keep the baby awake so that the last one-and-a-half hours of a three-hour cycle is the naptime. Also, check your milk supply. As we stated in Chapter 7, if your baby is hungry, feed him. But investigate why he is not reaching the minimum mark and start working toward it.

5. *Occasionally, just after I have fed, changed, and played with my new baby, I will put him down for a nap and within five minutes he starts crying—hard. This is unusual for him. What should I do?*

Go in and check on your baby. The fact that this is not routine behavior calls for your attention. He may have a messy diaper or need to be burped. Keep in mind that since it is naptime, some crying is not unusual. Napping is a skill that needs to be learned. Don't believe the myth that your baby is signaling a need to be picked up and rocked every time he cries.

6. *How much time is appropriate for holding my baby?*

Parents should be more concerned with what is an *inappropriate* amount of time to hold their baby, whether too little or too much. The latter is often the case with demand-feeding.

If you follow the parent-directed feeding plan, you will hold your baby the appropriate amount of time during the day without sacrificing your other areas of responsibility. The fact is, you hold your baby many times throughout the day during feeding, playing, loving, and diaper-changing times. Because you are following PDF, dad and other family members will also be holding and loving the baby.

7. *Sometimes, right after I feed my baby, she spits up what looks to be a good amount of the feeding. Should I feed her again right away?*

Even though your baby may seem to have lost her whole meal, normally you won't feed her again until her next routine feeding. The amount of partially digested milk regurgitated often appears to be greater than it actually is. Overfeeding and doing a poor job of burping a baby are common causes for projectile vomiting. However, if this problem continues routinely, it may signal a digestive problem. For your own peace of mind, and possibly for your baby's health, contact your pediatrician.

8. *My baby is eight weeks old and has not yet slept through the night. What should I do to eliminate the middle-of-the-night feeding?*

Go back and review the specific guidelines listed in Chapter 5. Are you following them? If so, your eight-week-old baby is ready to sleep through the night, for his sake and yours. If he is waking every night at basically the same time, then he is waking out of nighttime habit and not out of need. If that's the case, you may need to help him eliminate the feeding period by not physically attending to him. Normally it takes three nights of some crying before the habit is broken. He will never remember those three nights, nor will they have any negative effects on him. However, helping him to learn nighttime sleep behavior will have *positive* effects, and is healthier for both your baby and you.

9. *My three-month-old has been sleeping through the night for several weeks. But now she is starting to wake up during the night again. Why is this happening, and what should I do?*

This is not an uncommon event. Your baby is probably going through a growth spurt. For the next couple of days, add a feeding or two to her routine. If she is on a three-and-a-half- to four-hour schedule, go back to three hours between feedings for a portion of the daily routine. This situation is temporary, and will most likely be repeated in six months. It is also a prelude to your child's need for additional nutrition. Check with your pediatrician as to when your baby should start on cereal.

10. *I recently was at a family gathering and had just put the most popular guest (my baby daughter) down for a nap. She began to cry, and everyone looked to see what I would do. Aunt Martha volunteered to get the baby back up, and I reluctantly agreed to let her do it. What should I have done?*

Flexibility needs to be part of your plan. How old is the baby? How badly does she need to go down in a given instance? Be sensitive to the feelings of others. If you are characterized by following a schedule, allowing Aunt Martha to get the baby that one time will not hurt your baby's routine.

11. *My two-month-old has been sleeping through the night for five weeks, but last night he woke up at 3 A.M. What should I do when this happens?*

Since your baby has proven he is capable of sleeping through the night, we can rule out poor sleep-behavior training. Assess the situation. Is your baby too warm? Does he have a cold? Did the cat jump into the crib? Use good judgment when deciding what you are going to do. However, don't create wrong sleep patterns—by feeding your baby in the middle of the night—that will only need correcting three days later.

Chapter Thirteen

Principles for Starting Late

Unfortunately, not all parents start out with the advantages provided by the *BABYWISE* infant-management plan. Many awaken to the need after their babies are six, twelve, or eighteen months old and still are not sleeping through the night. Is it too late for these parents? Absolutely not. If you are in this situation and desire to correct the problem, the change must begin with you.

Below are some rules and guidelines that will help your baby establish continuous nighttime sleep.

General Rules

1. Make sure you have read and understand the entire contents of this book before proceeding any further.

2. Don't try to make any changes while out-of-town guests or relatives are visiting. You don't need the added pressure of explaining everything you are doing.

3. Start the process of change when your baby is healthy.

General Guidelines

1. Work on your baby's daytime routine for the first four to five days. Keep in mind the three activities you must include and their order—feeding time, waketime, then naptime. Review Chapter 7, "Establishing Your Baby's Routine," to determine how many feedings are appropriate in a twenty-four-hour period, given your child's age. For example, at three months of age your baby should be receiving four to five feedings a day. If he or she is six months old, your baby should be receiving three meals a day with a nursing period or a bottle just before bed.

If you have been in the habit of rocking or nursing your baby to sleep at naptime, now is the time to eliminate that practice.

2. Review Chapter 9, "When Your Baby Cries," and be prepared for some crying. You are moving from a high-comfort style of sleep manipulation to basic training in sleep skills. Initially, your baby will not like this change, but it's necessary.

In moments of parental stress, be comforted in knowing your baby won't feel abandoned because you have decided that the best thing for him is learning how to fall asleep on his own. Continue to think about and look toward the long-term benefits. Your proactive response is best for the baby, and for the entire family.

3. Don't feel the necessity to check on your baby every five minutes while he or she is crying. If you go into your baby's room, try to do so without being seen. If necessary, move the crib so you can see the baby but the baby can't see you. If you feel you must soothe the child, go in briefly and pat him or her on the back. With a soft voice, say, "It's all right," then quietly leave. As a result, your baby will do one of two things: be comforted and fall asleep, or roar even louder.

If your baby chooses the latter, don't be discouraged! The crying only means he or she has not yet developed the ability to settle himself or herself. That goal is precisely what you are working toward.

4. *Be patient and consistent.* For some parents, success comes after one night; for others, it comes after two weeks. The norm, however, is three to five days.

Summary

Retraining is always more difficult than training correctly from the start, but it needs to be done. Parents who love their babies give them what they need; young children need a good night's sleep.

Moms who have made the transition from sleepless nights to peaceful sleep report that their children not only gain the advantage of continuous nighttime sleep, but their daytime disposition also changes. They appear happier, more content, and definitely more manageable. We trust this will be the case with your baby.

We wish you and your family the best as you work at helping your child gain this fundamental skill—the ability to sleep, uninterrupted, right on through the night.

—Gary Ezzo and Dr. Robert Bucknam

Chapter Fourteen

Next Stop:
Babywise II

(Parenting Your Pretoddler, 5 to 15 Months)

T hroughout the process of your baby's growth, there are both constant and variable factors influencing development. As your child approaches the pretoddler stage, the variables of growth begin to play a more dominant role. How will you respond to those variables? Certainly not by abandoning that which has brought you so much success—your baby's routine. No, your child's routine is the foundation for healthy future development. You rightly respond to the emerging variables when you know in advance what to expect of your pretoddler, when to expect it, and at what ages different patterns of behavior normally emerge. Knowing what to look for enables a parent to set standards of expected behavior and provide the guidance needed to reach behavior-related goals.

What behavior *can* be expected of your pretoddler? Of what is he or she capable? *BABYWISE II* will emphasize the importance of learning patterns. Those patterns become models for learning that can assist the child throughout his or her early development. Just as cartilage strengthens and turns into bone during this period, learning patterns develop and form the infrastructure for future moral and academic learning. For this reason, the first patterns established should be the *right* patterns. *BABYWISE II* will help ensure that your child has a solid foundation for learning. The book is fun, informative, and most important, extremely practical.

For more information, write: *Growing Families International*, 9259 Eton Ave., Chatsworth, CA 91311.

Endnotes

Chapter 1. YOUR BABY NEEDS A FAMILY

1. The term "democratic parenting" was popularized in the mid-1940s by educational theorists Arnold Gesell and Rudolf Dreikurs.

2. The theory of democratic parenting is based on two assumptions: a) that a child has no natural propensity for wayward behavior, and b) that parental authority creates conflict. Therefore, the theory suggests that by eliminating or minimizing parental authority, parents can seriously reduce conflict in their child's life. This theory is overly optimistic.

Chapter 2. FEEDING PHILOSOPHIES

1. Dr. Rupert Rogers wrote on the problems of breast-feeding during the 1930s and 1940s. He told mothers to be old-fashioned. What did he mean by that? He said, go back to nursing periods arranged as follows: 6:00 A.M., 9:00 A.M., noon, 3:00 P.M., 6:00 P.M., and 10:00 P.M., and once when the baby woke in the night. Although that type of feeding was still a schedule, it wasn't referred to as such. The term "schedule" referred to a nursing technique more than a routine. *Mother's Encyclopedia* (New York: The Parents Institute, Inc., 1951), p. 122.

2. We don't take issue with a mother who chooses to breast-feed longer than a year because she enjoys that special time. We take issue with the suggestion that the child has a psychological need inherent at birth, and if not allowed access to his or her mother's breast, the child's future emotional health is put at risk.

Chapter 4. HUNGER AND SLEEP CYCLES

1. This conclusion was drawn from a study based on thirty-two mother-infant pairs observed over two years. Sixteen families were from the La Leche League, and the other sixteen were not. "Sleep-Wake Patterns of Breast-Fed Infants in the First Two Years of Life," *Pediatrics*, Vol. 77, No. 3, March 1986, p. 328.

2. Even as we write this edition, a two-month-old girl was smothered to death by her sleeping parent. (See "Baby dies after being hurt by dad accidentally," by Jeff Collins, Orange *County Register*, Santa Ana, Calif., February 23, 1994.) For a Consumer Product Safety warning about the potential danger of taking an infant of less than one year of age into the bed of a parent, see "The Family Bed," by Loci De Noxa, *Owings Mills Times*, Maryland, March 31, 1994, p. 25.

Chapter 5. FACTS ON FEEDING

1. A baby's immune system is developed by two means. During pregnancy, disease-fighting proteins called antibodies pass from the mother's blood to the baby's blood. They provide temporary protection against the many illnesses to which the mother has been exposed. After birth, the baby's immune system is enhanced with breast milk. That is done two ways: 1) by the passing of the mother's antibodies through the milk, which are then absorbed into the child's bloodstream; and 2) by way of the *bifidus factor*. Infants are born with millions of tiny organisms in a semidormant state, which are members of the *Lactobacillus-bifidus* family. Their growth is stimulated by certain elements in the mother's milk. As these organisms grow, they

produce acetic and lactic acids that prevent the growth of many disease-producing organisms, such as E. coli and dysentery bacilli. This does not mean that bottle-fed babies have no immune system; they do, but it is not as protective.

2. Breast-feeding mothers are sometimes warned not to use a bottle. The concern is over "nipple confusion." The belief is that a baby will become confused and refuse the breast if offered a bottle. Although under normal circumstances there will be no need to introduce a bottle to the breast-fed infant in the first month, there will come a time when the bottle will be a welcome friend. The bottle allows other family members to share in the joy of feeding the newest family member. Though babies don't become confused over nipples, they may demonstrate a preference for one over another. You can guide their choice.

Chapter 9. WHEN YOUR BABY CRIES

1. Crying periods vary with each child. When you include his or her late-afternoon fussy time, a normal baby may cry as much as three hours total per day, with five to forty-five minutes in any one session.

Chapter 11. PARENTING POTPOURRI: TOPICS OF INTEREST TO NEW PARENTS

1. Michael E. Lamb, Ph.D., from the Department of Pediatrics at the University of Utah Medical School, summarizes our position: "The preponderance of the evidence thus suggests that extended

contact [the bonding theory] has no clear effects on maternal behavior," *Pediatrics*, Vol. 70, No. 5, November 1982, p. 768.

Subject Index

Notes

Notes

Notes

....

Notes

Notes

....

Notes

Notes

Notes

Notes

Notes

Notes

Notes

....